Out of Harm's Way:
Readings on Child Sexual Abuse, Its Prevention and Treatment

Edited by Dawn C. Haden

ORYX PRESS
1986

The rare Arabian Oryx is believed to have inspired the myth of the unicorn. This desert antelope became virtually extinct in the early 1960s. At that time several groups of international conservationists arranged to have 9 animals sent to the Phoenix Zoo to be the nucleus of a captive breeding herd. Today the Oryx population is over 400, and herds have been returned to reserves in Israel, Jordan, and Oman.

Library of Congress Cataloging-in-Publication Data

Out of harm's way.

    Articles reprinted from various publications.
    Bibliography: p.
    Includes index.
    1. Child molesting—United States. 2. Child molesting—United States—Prevention. 3. Sexually abused children—United States. I. Haden, Dawn C. [DNLM: 1. Child Abuse—collected works. 2. Child Abuse—prevention & control—collected works. 3. Sex Offenses—collected works. WA 320 094]
HQ72.U53095 1986   362.7′044   86-42783
ISBN 0-89774-311-3

Table of Contents

Preface

Child sexual abuse is a harsh reality of the present age. Our society has attempted to clean its closets of all the problems that are surrounded by social taboos, but child sexual abuse has been the most difficult for us to uncover. Unlike our predecessors, however, we have decided to meet the challenge by creating public awareness. In this way, we can begin the complex task of aiding those who have been damaged by it, protecting those who could be its potential victims, and dealing constructively with its perpetrators. As with any societal ill, there are not, nor ever will be, any quick solutions or easy answers to the many questions surrounding the problem. The responsibilities of dealing with child sexual abuse are awesome, but the consequences of ignoring it are no longer acceptable; they can only perpetuate it.

Statistics indicate that the problem is widespread. They should serve to warn all who are concerned with the well-being of children that new strategies must be developed and implemented to protect children against the potential of being sexually abused. But what are some of these strategies and who is responsible for teaching them? The parent? The educator? How is public and parental consciousness being raised, and is it possible to make inroads into significantly decreasing this problem?

The child who has experienced the trauma of sexual abuse must be able to find caring adults who offer genuine support and knowledgeable concern. This is primary for enabling these youngsters to rebuild their self-esteem and exonerate any misplaced guilt. Researchers have determined that sexually abused children often exhibit certain telling, behavioral characteristics. What are the evidences that a child's caretaker should be looking for and what are the sequential steps for reporting suspected abuse? Are there any "better" or "best" ways of helping the abused child? What professionals should become involved and who should be the one primarily responsible for helping the child?

Although it is difficult to maintain perspective in the midst of a crisis caused by the sexual abuse of a child, it is imperative that all issues be handled knowledgeably so that the child is protected from any further physical or psychological harm. Legally, there are also important considerations; among these are preserving the rights of individuals, videotape testimony, the child as a witness, and most important, procedures for reporting suspected sexual abuse. What, then, are the legal ramifications of these questions and what procedures are best implemented when reporting these cases?

An objective examination of the abusers is also imperative when making any purposeful attempt at eliminating the root of the problem. Do they share any commonalities? Is there a typical profile of an abuser? Were child abusers themselves abused as children? What is the prognosis for their "recovery"? Can incestuous families be rebuilt and turned around to form "healthy" families? These and the other questions above are some of those that must be explored to reach the goal of freeing children from the heinous burden of sexual abuse.

The central purpose of this reader is to offer perspectives on the parameters of child sexual abuse. It can also aid in building children's defenses. The articles included give a sense of the complexity of the problem and establish guidelines for beginning to find the answers to the many questions posed above. There are many caring, responsible adults who interact with children; these can include parents, educators, social workers, psychologists, physicians, and/or attorneys. Each has an area of expertise, and the informed, up-to-date, knowledgeable blending of these talents is the best course for both defense and recovery.

This volume is divided into five sections. The opening section provides the reader with an overview of the problem. Methods and programs for developing children's defenses against sexual abuse are contained in the second section. Articles in the third section discuss identifying the abused child and the various programs throughout the country that have been implemented to offer assistance. The fourth section covers legal considerations and responsibilities as well as the issues confronting the variety of professionals involved with sexually abused children. The final section describes the abuser.

Three appendices follow the text. Appendix A is an annotated bibliography of print materials in two sections: for use by adults and for use with children. Appendix B is a listing of audiovisual materials available for use with children. Appendix C is a selective list of the major agencies and organizations which provide help in preventing child sexual abuse, counseling to abused children and their families, and legal advice.

One closing comment: An attempt was made when selecting articles to avoid those that centered around particular incidences of abuse in order to maintain objectivity and give a clearer purpose to the discussion of this "delicate" subject. It is hoped that readers of this book will emerge with a power that can only come through a real understanding of the problem of sexual abuse; a power to make changes for all children; a power to keep them out of harm's way.

SECTION I

Seeking Parameters: An Overview

Introduction

When beginning the study of any problem it is essential to first measure the problem's dimensions. The two articles in this section introduce the reader to the broad spectrum that child sexual abuse encompasses and survey society's involvement in its treatment and prevention.

The opening article, "How Widespread Is Child Sexual Abuse?," by Dr. David Finkelhor, outlines the difficulties of assessing the parameters of child sexual abuse and draws attention to the complexities that are involved in compiling any meaningful statistics. Julie Wang, in her article "Child Abuse Alert!," highlights the role that the media has played in raising the public consciousness of the crime of child sexual abuse and provides an overview of society's growing response to this problem.

How Widespread Is Child Sexual Abuse?

by David Finkelhor

Starting in the mid-1970s, child welfare professionals began to notice a dramatic increase in the number of cases of child abuse that involved some kind of sexual exploitation. As such cases continued to mushroom in the late 1970s, these professionals were joined by journalists, publishers and film producers who also became alarmed about the problem.

Soon the public was being exposed to a wave of books, magazine articles and television programs describing or, in many cases, graphically portraying this disturbing type of child abuse.

People at all levels, from politicians and policymakers to informed newspaper readers, came to know that child sexual abuse is one of the most serious forms of child abuse and much more common than was once thought. But exactly how common is it?

Everyone has heard figures: half of all girls, one in four girls, one in 10 boys. Where do these figures come from? Is sexual abuse really this widespread?

Unfortunately, there are no precise and reliable figures on the incidence of child sexual abuse in the United States. And there may never be. By its very nature, sexual abuse is a problem that is concealed. Gathering statistics about it is a frustrating and precarious undertaking. So the cases actually uncovered by statisticians and researchers may represent only a tip of an unfathomable iceberg.

Nonetheless, several efforts have been made to try to gauge the extent of sexual abuse. Some of these attempts have come much closer to the truth than anyone expected.

David Finkelhor is the Associate Director of the Family Violence Research Program, University of New Hampshire. "How Widespread Is Child Sexual Abuse?" is reprinted from *Children Today,* July/August 1984, volume 13, number 4, pp. 18–20. Reprinted by permission of the author.

The American Humane Association (AHA) publishes nationwide statistics on child abuse and neglect. These figures are collected from the 50 states, which in turn get their figures each year by counting the cases that were officially reported to each state's child protection authorities.

AHA's tally of sexual abuse cases reached a high of 22,918 in 1982, the most recent year for which statistics have been assembled.[1]

Although this figure is 10 times larger than the 1,975 cases of sexual abuse tallied in 1976, the first year of AHA's collection effort, everyone recognizes that even 22,918 is a drastic undercount. It is well known to professionals in the field that a great number of sexual abuse cases are never officially reported and thus would not be included in the AHA count.

To try to improve upon these figures, the National Center for Child Abuse and Neglect (NCCAN) commissioned an even more comprehensive study of the incidence of child abuse and neglect.[2] In the National Incidence study, conducted in 1979, 26 counties in 10 states were chosen as representative of the country. By using a toll-free telephone number and confidential questionnaires distributed to agencies throughout these counties, researchers hoped to find out about cases that were known to professionals but had not been officially reported.

Extrapolating from the 26 counties to the nation as a whole, the National Incidence study estimated that 44,700 cases of sexual abuse were known to professionals in the year beginning April 1979. The researchers figured that their procedures uncovered almost twice as many cases as would have been known to the official reporting agencies alone.

Although 44,700 cases of sexual abuse in a single year is a serious problem, even this figure is still considered a gross underestimate. What is missing is information on all the abuse that occurs but is not known to any agency or professional at all. This abuse is known only to victims and perpetrators and, perhaps, to a few family members and friends. This abuse may well constitute the majority.

SURVEYING VICTIMS

To try to find out the scope of this unreported abuse, several researchers have taken another approach. They have tried to ask victims directly. Unfortunately, there are problems to asking such questions of children who are currently victims. Parents would be unlikely to give permission to interview them, and children might be put in danger of retaliation if they did tell.

So, removing themselves one step, researchers have interviewed adults about sexual abuse that may have happened to them when they were children.

One of the first researchers to take this approach was Alfred Kinsey in his famous study of female sexuality.[3] Kinsey and workers asked 4,441 female subjects if they had ever been "approached while they were preadolescent by adult males who appeared to be making sexual advances, or who had made sexual contacts." Twenty-four percent said such a thing had happened to them. This is the source of a widely quoted statistic that one in four women are sexually abused.

There are several important facts to note about Kinsey's estimate. For one thing, more than half of the experiences the women in his study reported involved contacts with exhibitionists only. For another, his figures do not include any experiences occurring to adolescent girls or any abuse at the hands of offenders who were not adults.

Another estimate about sexual abuse based on adults reporting about their childhood comes from a study conducted by this writer, who asked 796 students at six New England colleges and universities to fill out questionnaires about childhood sexual experiences of all types.[4]

Sexual victimization was defined as a sexual experience between a child 12 or under with a partner at least five years older, or between a child 13 to 16 with a partner at least 10 years older. By this definition, 19 percent of the women (approximately one in five) and nine percent of the men (about one in 11) had been sexually victimized. About 20 percent of the experiences were with exhibitionists.

One defect of both this and the Kinsey studies is that they did not use samples that were representative—Kinsey's respondents were all volunteers, and mine were all students. However, three other studies of the prevalence of sexual abuse have been done using more systematic samples.

In 1980, Glenn Kercher, a researcher at Sam Houston State University, and colleagues mailed out questionnaires to 2,000 people randomly selected from all those who held Texas drivers' licenses.[5] In reply to one question, which asked whether the person had ever been a victim of sexual abuse as a child, 12 percent of the females and three percent of the males—of a total of 1,054 respondents—admitted they had been sexually abused.

Under a grant from the National Center for Prevention and Control of Rape, I conducted another study, a household survey of a representative sample of 521 adults in the Boston metropolitan area, all of whom were the parents of children between the ages of six and 14.[6] The adults were asked about sexual experiences they had had when they were children, prior to age 16, with a person at least five years older, which they themselves considered to have been abuse.

Under this definition of sexual abuse, 15 percent of the women and five percent of the men had been sexually abused.

The study that has found the highest rate of sexual abuse was one conducted by sociologist Diana Russell, also under a grant from the National Center for Prevention and Control of Rape, who interviewed a random sample of 933 adult women in San Francisco in 1978 about a wide variety of sexual assault experiences.[7] She found that 38 percent of these women had had a sexual abuse experience involving physical contact before they were 18. If non-contact experiences—like encounters with exhibitionists and unwanted advances—were included, the figure rose to 54 percent.

That Russell's figures are so much higher than those of other studies may be attributed in part to the thoroughness of her questions. Where other studies asked adults a single question about sexual abuse, Russell asked 14 separate questions about sexually exploitative experiences, any one of which may have reminded people about some sexual abuse that occurred in their childhood. She also included abusive experiences at the hands of peers in her definition of sexual abuse.

IMPLICATIONS

These surveys have added greatly to our knowledge about child sexual abuse. They have shown that the experience of being molested occurs to an alarming number of children and that both boys and girls are victims. They have also shown that most victims do not tell anyone, confirming the suspicion that reported cases are only a tip of the iceberg.

Unfortunately, these surveys have not given us a definitive figure for how many children are sexually abused in the United States. Russell's findings cannot be used to say that "more than one out of every two girls is molested," nor could my findings be used to argue that 15 percent of all girls and five percent of all boys are sexually abused.

For one thing, these studies are local and cannot be generalized to the country as a whole. For another, they are studies of adults and we do not know for sure that the current generation of children is having the same experience.

They can be used, however, as general guides for how widespread the problem of victimization probably is. In answering the question about the prevalence of sexual abuse, it is fair to say that "studies of various groups of adults looking back on their childhoods have found that anywhere from nine to 54 percent of the women and three to nine percent of the men were sexually abused."

REFERENCES

1. American Humane Association, *The National Study on Child Neglect and Abuse Reporting,* Denver, AHA, 1982.

2. National Center for Child Abuse and Neglect, *Study Findings: National Study of the Incidence and Severity of Child Abuse and Neglect,* Washington, DHHS, 1981.

3. A. Kinsey, et al., *Sexual Behavior in the Human Female,* Philadelphia, Saunders, 1953.

4. D. Finkelhor, *Sexually Victimized Children,* New York, Free Press, 1979.

5. G. Kercher, *Responding to Child Sexual Abuse, A Report to the 67th Session of the Texas Legislature,* Huntsville, Tex., Sam Houston State University, 1980.

6. D. Finkelhor, *Child Sexual Abuse: New Theory and Research,* New York, Free Press, (in press).

7. D. Russell, "The Incidence and Prevalence of Intrafamilial and Extrafamilial Sexual Abuse of Female Children," *Child Abuse and Neglect,* 7, 1983.

Child Abuse Alert!

by Julie Wang

Of all the crimes ever conceived or committed, none inspires more revulsion and disbelief than the sexual abuse of children by adults—a subject that has received unrelenting national coverage in recent months. In one front-page story, U.S. Senator [Paula] Hawkins of Florida told a shocked audience at the Third National Conference on Sexual Victimization of Children in Washington, DC, how a neighborhood babysitter—a known, respected "man around the corner"—had sexually abused her as a child, a fact she had never until that moment revealed to anyone except her mother. She recounted how he had lured kids with toys and candy, and how she eventually served as witness at his trial, an experience she still remembers with "horror." But because the presiding judge decided that she and other children were simply lying, he dismissed the case and the man was set free.

In fact, the reality of child abuse is so unsettling that adults—law enforcement officials, therapists, parents—often choose to deny or ignore the warning signals that tell of molestation by an adult caretaker or incest within the home. "Sexual abuse has always been one of the most *under-reported* forms of child abuse in our society," confirms Martha Kendrick, social science analyst at the National Center on Child Abuse and Neglect in Washington.

But slowly and dramatically the "conspiracy of silence" surrounding sexual crimes against minors is being shattered. No longer can people dismiss such cases as isolated aberrations primarily affecting low-income and rural families. Since 1976, reports of the problem have more than doubled. And in perhaps the most chilling statement of all, Senator Christopher J. Dodd of Connecticut, co-chairman of the Senate Children's Caucus, has declared that even by "the most conservative estimates," a child is sexually abused somewhere in the

U.S. every two minutes, and that one in five victims is under the age of seven. Even months-old infants are not spared, he reveals.

While a seeming epidemic of abuse prevails, much is being done in terms of prevention, protection and treatment. Here's what's happening around the country.

MEDIA'S ROLE

That sexual abuse can and often does occur within attractive, upper middle class families was the message of the recent prime-time ABC-TV special *Something About Amelia,* scheduled to be rebroadcast in the near future.

This much-talked-about drama portrayed a fairly typical example of a girl abused by her father, according to Dr. Stan J. Katz, clinical psychologist at the Children's Institute International in Los Angeles, who served as technical adviser to the filmmakers.

At first, when Amelia makes her accusation, she is not believed, and the initial shock of the revelation is turned into anger toward her for making such "disgusting" allegations. In the film, the father eventually admits his crime and is removed from the home but kept out of jail. Amelia is temporarily separated from her parents and the entire family receives counseling. Although the movie suggests that they will ultimately be reunited, this may be an idealized version of what actually takes place, says Dr. Katz. In reality, about half the families split up within a year after the father admits to incest.

Other media efforts in the campaign against sexual abuse have featured actress Lindsay Wagner, the former "Bionic Woman" who played a leading role this past May in *Touch,* a half-hour teleplay produced by the Minneapolis Illusion Theater. (The group specializes in dramas that portray the realities of "everyday" child molestation involving family members or trusted caretakers from outside the home.)

An NBC Boston affiliate, WBZ-TV, recently showed *This Secret Should Be Told* in which a therapist/ventriloquist and her puppet characters, a (boy) lion and a (girl) duck, encourage young viewers to tell a concerned adult should anyone fondle them in an unnatural way.

Still another media creation—this time a 30-minute home audiotape—is *Hands-Off Bill,* a character conceived by ex-policeman Lloyd Martin who once directed the sexually exploited child unit of the Los Angeles Police Department. Bill, speaking with the voice of a little boy, talks to children in a radio-show-format highlighted by prerecorded interviews with those who call in to discuss their experiences. The tape comes with a workbook designed for children. After completing it, they can receive a certificate stating, "This special person has permission to say *no* to uncomfortable touching and will tell." A child who learns to refuse an adult's sexual advances firmly is believed to be better protected, as studies have shown that many would-be molesters back away in such situations.

CRIMINAL JUSTICE & LEGAL TRENDS

According to a report issued by the National Center on Child Abuse and Neglect, a federally funded bureau in Washington, DC (based on 14 model projects across the U.S.), it is very difficult to prosecute offenders unless child-protective services cooperate closely with law-enforcement officers. (When they do present a united front in court, it is virtually impossible for the abuser to defend himself successfully, one project director observes.)

In cases of incest, all authorities emphasize the necessity of relying on the clout of the legal system to keep families committed to a distressing, painful and time-consuming treatment process. In such situations, therapy is most successful when the parent involved admits to the crime, is legally punished for it and the spouse believes the abuse has occurred, thereby supporting the child.

Unfortunately, the reality is that successful criminal prosecution of sexual abuse is still the exception rather than the rule. For one thing, child-care professionals, including doctors, nurses, social workers and teachers, often fail to abide by legal mandates that require them to report suspected cases to local authorities. Sometimes this may be done for reasons of confidentiality—especially with "respected" members of a community, for example. Other times, medical and social personnel may refrain from acting out of fear or confusion regarding the unwieldly legal process itself.

This year, New York City will introduce a bill in the State Legislature compelling all such professionals to demonstrate a basic knowledge of child abuse laws *before* being eligible for licenses to practice. (Right now, anyone within the state, concerned professional or not, who wishes to report a suspicious case can call the New York State Central Register, 1-800-342-3720.)

But even the fact that a case is recorded and brought to court does not necessarily guarantee that justice will be served. Of those arrested in the U.S. on child-sex charges, an estimated 95 per cent never receive a prison sentence, reports Irving Prager, associate professor of law at the University of LaVerne College of Law, Children's Justice Center, CA. And a recent annual survey shows that only 162 out of 30,000 child molesters nationwide spent time either in a prison or state mental hospital.

Why such a dismal record? Largely because the legal system has traditionally demanded corroboration before admitting a child's testimony as evidence. Since adults are not likely to commit such sexual crimes in public, this documentation was usually impossible to provide, and prosecutors could do nothing to protect the child from further abuse. New York State's Governor Cuomo has now signed a bill dropping the requirement for confirmation, and other states are expected to follow suit.

Yet even this legislation may be circumvented since the trial and cross-examination can be a grueling ordeal for any child. The attorney or psychiatrist for the defense may try to convince a jury that he or she is making up stories and a parade of witnesses may be brought in to vouch for the upstanding moral character of the accused—thereby pitting the youngster's word against many. In addition, the questioning itself can prove intimidating as the attorney tries to uncover inconsistencies or exaggerations in a child's statements. One case in Georgia was dismissed when a judge decided that the victim's use of the phrase "millions of times" to describe how often the defendant had molested her constituted hyperbole, which he felt discredited *all* her previous testimony!

To help monitor court proceedings and press for harsher laws and stiffer sentences, several parent groups have organized, among them, SLAM: Concerned Citizens For Stronger Legislation Against Molesters, founded by the grandmother of a little girl who was raped and murdered by a repeat sex offender. (The latter had shortly before been released from a state mental hospital, labeled "cured.") Judges are presumably aware that the very presence of such vocal groups in the courtroom may lead to front-page newspaper stories if the child abuser is let off too lightly.

Crisis Intervention

Sexual abuse often presents itself as an immediate crisis situation when victims—desperately traumatized or terrified of returning home—may show up, sometimes with a relative or friend, in hospital emergency rooms. Most city hospitals have social workers on their staffs who are trained to recognize and treat molested children.

Among the intervention programs for battered and/or sexually mistreated children is the crisis nursery at the New York City Foundling Hospital, whose medical director, Dr. Vincent J. Fontana, is also chairman of the Mayor's Task Force on Child Abuse and Neglect. This crisis service includes a toll-free, round-the-clock parent helpline that can stave off impending incidents as well as handle emergencies after the fact. A similar Manhattan facility is the Presbyterian Hospital's Therapeutic Nursery.

Branches of the various Junior Leagues across the U.S. sponsor rape-counseling groups, hotlines for reporting sexual abuse and domestic violence shelters. The St. Louis branch of the Leagues funded a pilot project for counseling mothers and daughters involved with incest. The pilot was so successful it is being continued by the Family and Children's Service of St. Louis under the name of New Foundations.

Right after airing *Something About Amelia,* the National Association of Social Workers, in cooperation with ABC, answered telephones at local network affiliates around the country to tap viewer response and handle emergency calls. As predicted, hundreds of requests from victims and concerned relatives of the abused were answered and counseling referrals were made. The NASW, with 55 chapters coast to coast, now broadcasts public service announcements, including information on how to get help, on public radio stations.

Family Therapy

The 14 projects authorized by the National Center on Child Abuse and Neglect, offer a wide range of treatments, found both necessary and helpful to all members of a family trying to cope with either incest or sexual assault by an outside party.

The therapies are often based on a crisis intervention approach—letting family members air their feelings in a nonjudgmental environment, social work counseling, individual, group and family therapy and, in some cases, marriage counseling to help reunite the parents constructively. Improving communication among family members and teaching parenting skills are also of central importance.

Pioneering a new, more multifaceted approach to treatment for incest, Dr. Hank Giarretto, Ph.D., a California-based family therapist who runs the Child Sexual Abuse Treatment Program (CSATP) in Santa Clara County, shows therapists how to coordinate the various state and city agencies to obtain the best treatment for both victim and offender.

According to Dr. Giarretto, "The child's overwhelming fear is that by revealing the dread secret, she has placed her father and family in serious jeopardy and betrayed her mother." Thus, the first step in dealing with the emotional overlay of incest is to reestablish a mother-daughter bond. The mother must side with the child in believing what has happened. Very often mothers deny the reality of sexual abuse because it points to a deep-seated problem between husband and wife.

"When the father is prosecuted and sentenced, counseling for the child begins almost immediately, helping her realize that she was indeed victimized at home, and that it was her mother's duty to take or agree to this action in order to protect her." (Experience has shown that the youngster must hear this not only from the therapist but also convincingly from the mother before she'll be psychologically receptive to treatment.)

"Although we. . .try to reunite families whenever possible rather than break them up irrevocably, change is a very slow and delicate process. The father should *not* be brought back in unless we can be reasonably sure that the situation will not repeat itself, and that the family—including the father—will accept ongoing professional help," warns Dr. Reese Abright, chief of child and adolescent psychiatry at St. Vincent's Hospital in New York City.

Group Therapies

Among the various treatment components that make up the CSATP is *Parents United,* (a self-help group), which now has 40 chapters in California alone and 89 around the country. The organization's activities include group therapy between couples, a coed and separate men's and women's groups, programs to help molested children, and also one focusing specifically on social skills to help offenders and victims, many of whom are loners, cope successfully with society once again.

Daughters and Sons United deals with children five to 18 years old. Treatment aims to alleviate trauma and feelings of guilt. Among adolescents the emphasis is on preventing subsequent destructive behavior, such as running away, heavy drug use, promiscuity, prostitution and suicide. Therapists also try to prevent repeated abuse by increasing the victim's independence and self-esteem.

Finally, *Adults Molested As Children United* helps women and men come to terms with sexual attacks that happened long ago, which have undermined their ability to form lasting, healthy relationships. Only by working through their anger, betrayal and sense of abandonment can such individuals ever learn to lead productive lives.

Another self-help group, Formerly Abused Children Emerging in Society (FACES), in Manchester, CT, provides ongoing support for young adults from abusive backgrounds who have recurring problems. According to co-founder, Lorraine Hovey-Rowe, they are often reluctant to become parents themselves, for fear of perpetuating the cycle. Yet they find themselves mistreating those they love—brothers, sisters, friends, even pets.

FACES members work on overcoming their feelings of isolation, on building up trust in both others and themselves and a sense of self-worth. Often they must conquer intense rage against parents who either maltreated them or were unable to protect them from hurt. "Their anger isn't hurting their parents, but it is crippling *them,*" says

Ann L. Bonney, the other co-founder of FACES and a child life specialist at the Manchester Memorial Hospital.

Play Therapy

One of the more intriguing therapies to emerge from the publicity surrounding the disclosure of sexual child abuse at the McMartin Preschool in Manhattan Beach, CA, was the use of puppets to help children act out their fears and demonstrate the outrages they suffered.

Kee MacFarlane, who directs the Child Abuse Diagnostic Center at Children's Institute International in Los Angeles, a United Way agency, and who served for six years as a specialist with the National Center on Child Abuse and Neglect, found that children who were afraid to recount what happened to them were frequently willing to let hand puppets "tell" their secrets. MacFarlane is credited with exposing the McMartin scandal as a result of her persistent "play therapy."

Spider-Man to the Rescue

In a new approach to focus attention on sexual abuse and teach children how to protect themselves, Margaret M. Heckler, Secretary of the U.S. Department of Health & Human Services, recently joined forces with Marvel Comics' most popular superhero as well as the National Committee for Prevention of Child Abuse in Chicago. The result is a special comic book scheduled for release by September that will feature both Spider-Man and Power Pack, a new generation of super-heroes, showing how children can protect themselves against sexually abusive adults.

In one episode, after a young boy is approached by his babysitter, Spider-Man reveals that he went through a similar incident himself as a child. In another lifelike scenario, the Power Pack lend their support to a young girl whose father has abused her.

"We are very pleased to be developing this project with Marvel," says Anne H. Cohn, D.P.H., executive director of the National Committee. "We believe that a comic book utilizing such popular figures will help us communicate effectively with our target audience," she adds. "Many children are more likely to pick up and read through a comic book and to absorb messages they might ignore from our sources."

Educational Materials

In a staged presentation, one of the most creative preventive efforts being introduced, a space woman named "Bub" comes down to earth and is helped out of her bubble spacecraft by two humans, Archie and Betty. Bub is like people in every way, except that she does not understand the sense of touch. This gives Archie and Betty an ideal opportunity to teach Bub the meaning of "good" and "bad" kinds of touching.

Performed as participatory theater in area public schools by the Kansas City, KS Junior League, the play, *The Bubbylonian Experience,* is also available as a film and comes with a manual to explain to community groups how to prepare themselves before showing it to young children. One chapter of the Junior Leagues has even videotaped the play to teach Girl Scout and Brownie groups about self-protection from sexual abuse.

"We've found that in schools where we've performed, the play has encouraged children to speak out about their own experiences," says Gloria Shearer, president-elect of the Kansas City branch. "Some people have wondered if we're just triggering the children's imagination, but in every case we've discovered that the situation is a real one, not simply a fantasy on the child's part."

Published books and manuals have proliferated in order to raise awareness of the problem's magnitude and show families and children how to protect themselves. For example, *Breaking The Cycle of Child Abuse* (Winston Press, MN) by Christine Comstock Herbruck, executive director of Parents Anonymous, a national organization based in Torrance, CA, reports how a group of troubled, abusive parents, who were themselves molested as children, band together to learn new alternatives to help break the cycle.

Hope For The Children, another Winston Press book, relates the personal history of Parents Anonymous, highlighting the backgrounds of several child abusers who choose to face and work through their problems. (The organization is now developing a nationwide children's treatment program so that communities will have information on how to establish very low-cost, high-quality services for abused children and teens.)

Still another new book, *Your Children Should Know,* dealing with self-protection, is co-authored by Tamar Hosansky, one of the founders of New York's Safety and Fitness Exchange.

A battery of books, pamphlets and leaflets are also offered by the American Humane Association in Denver, CO, including publications aimed at social work professionals, parents and schools. In addition, the Association issues, free, *The National Child Protective Services Newsletter,* a quarterly report, and a leaflet called *Stop! Don't Hurt Me!* that answers basic questions asked by children about child neglect and abuse. They include a hotline number and protective services information upon request.

While all such developments are encouraging, it is you the parent who bears the ultimate responsibility for your child's safety and well-being. That means educating your son and daughter, investigating child-care facilities and schools thoroughly and staying alert to all the signals, both outside and within the home, that point to possible sexual misconduct by an adult.

SECTION II

Prevention of Sexual Abuse

Introduction

Society's dedication to the old adage "an ounce of prevention is worth a pound of cure" is nowhere more apparent than in the area of child sexual abuse. Recent media attention to this problem has created a proliferation of prevention programs and literature which are all designed, in one way or another, to sharpen children's defenses against abuse.

Lisa Wilson Strick, in her article "How to Protect Your Child from Sexual Assault," focuses on the parental responsibilities involved in teaching children how to avoid sexual abuse. Emphasis on helping children build their defenses against sexual assault is also covered in Susan Newman's article "Turning Away Exploitation," where she outlines parental strategies for creating children's awareness of their rights to the privacy of their own bodies.

In "Confronting a Near and Present Danger," Sally Cooper describes the Child Assault Prevention workshops where role-playing teaches children how to resist assault. The importance of developing a child's ability to identify danger and to give him/her coping strategies to deal with a threatening situation are also explained.

Good books provide another vehicle for prevention in "Sexual Abuse: Teaching about Touching." Margo Hittleman, in her article by that name, evaluates the use of books in sexual abuse prevention and includes an annotated bibliography for use by both children and adults.

The section closes with a federal government publication made available through the Office of Human Development Services entitled "Child Sexual Abuse Prevention." This checklist gives guidelines for parents for (1) establishing clear lines of communication with their children for the purpose of preventing abuse, (2) choosing a reliable day care center in which to entrust the care of their child, and (3) knowing what symptoms to look for and measures to take if abuse has occurred.

How to Protect Your Child from Sexual Assault

by Lisa Wilson Strick

A week before Emily started kindergarten her mother had a talk with her about strangers. "You must never take candy or presents from strange men, honey," she said. "Sometimes bad men like to hurt little girls. If a strange man asks you to get into a car with him or anything like that, you mustn't do it. A bad man might even ask you to take your clothes off so he can touch you. That's wrong and you should never agree to such a thing. You can scream or run away."

Emily was quiet.

"Do you understand, honey?"

"Yes," said the five-year-old. "You mean don't take anything from strangers."

"That's right. What else?"

"Don't talk to bad men. Don't let bad men touch me."

"Good! You're a big girl, and now you know the rules!"

Satisfied that she had done a proper job of warning her daughter about the ugly possibility of child molestation, Emily's mother relaxed. She was totally unprepared for the child's next question:

"Mommy, you said I shouldn't let bad men touch me. But when Grandpa wants me to take off my pants and sit on his lap, is that OK?"

The instruction given Emily on sexual assault is typical of that offered to most children today. We warn our children about the stranger near the schoolyard, the man with candy in his pocket or a present in his car, the man who wants to "show you something special." This advice is sometimes reinforced in classrooms by teachers or social workers or police officers. Most grade-school children can recite the standard "Stranger-Danger" lecture by heart.

Typical also is the shock a parent experiences on learning that her child is being sexually exploited not by a stranger, but by a person close to or in the family. The sad truth is, however, that the great majority of sexually abused children are assaulted by people they know and trust. As Emily's mother found out, parents who lecture school-age children about strangers and then drop the subject are offering too little—and sometimes offering it too late.

The way parents approach sexual assault has not changed much in a generation—a fact that reflects widespread misunderstanding of the problem. In some ways this is not surprising; the subject is so disturbing that people don't like to think about it, much less discuss it openly. But if children are to be protected the facts must be faced. Sexual assault of children is on the rise. Up to 790,000 cases are now reported in the United States each year—and most experts agree that this is a vastly under-reported crime. One of every five rape victims is under twelve. The great majority of offenders are male, but boys as well as girls are attacked. Victims have included toddlers and even infants.

Less than one third of recorded assaults on children are committed by strangers. Usually the victim knows her assailant well. At least 30 percent of the time the child molester is a relative. (Many experts think the percentage is much higher, but because incestuous incidents are the least likely to be reported, it is difficult to demonstrate this statistically.)

"It isn't that the evil stranger on the corner doesn't exist," says Patricia Fletcher, executive director of the Rape Crisis Center of Syracuse, New York, an agency that handled over two hundred cases of sexual assault on children last year. "It's just that children have a lot less to fear from him than they do from relatives, neighbors and so-called friends. Very often sexual abuse begins disguised as playful or affectionate contact and progresses from there. Eventually the situation becomes frightening, physically uncomfortable or painful. But by then the child may have been locked into the abusive relationship so long that she feels she can't refuse. Some children are repeatedly assaulted for years and never report it."

According to Dr. Debrah A. Shulman, a psychologist in Fayetteville, New York, who works extensively with young people, "Children want and need physical contact. It's as basic as the need for food. An unhealthy person can exploit that need for his own gratification. If the exploiter is someone the child looks up to and trusts—a father, for example—the child's perception of human relationships can become terribly distorted. The psychological damage suffered by such a child may be far greater than the physical harm inflicted."

Suzanne Spier, coordinator for Alliance, a private agency in Syracuse, New York, that provides a variety of services for abused children and their families, agrees: "A high percentage of deeply troubled teenagers—runaways, drug and alcohol addicts, attempted suicides—were sexually abused as children. The exploitation of many of the kids we see started as early as age five or six. A child of this age may submit to confusing or uncomfortable 'games' simply to please an adult who is important to her or him. If coaxing fails, bribery or a threat may be used to secure the child's participation."

Offenders often use "psychological blackmail" to prevent children from reporting what is going on. When the assailant is a relative, he can often insure silence by associating disclosure with breaking up the family. "I was abused by my stepfather for four years, starting when I was six," reports one victim, now in her twenties. "He said that if I ever told anybody about it, the police would come get him and my mother would lose her job. The family would starve and it would all be my fault." The abuse of this child ended only when her mother's marriage broke up and her stepfather moved away. Another victim, assaulted repeatedly by her father, kept quiet because "he said that if I ever told, he would put my mother against a wall and shoot her." She'd seen her father abuse her mother and believed he would carry out his threat.

Many people think that sexual abuse of children doesn't happen in "nice" neighborhoods. Incest, in particular, is commonly thought to predominate at lower socio-economic levels. But as many incidents of incest are reported from affluent suburban communities as from slums. There is no typical offender. The child molester is as likely to be a professional man or an executive as an unskilled or unemployed worker. Child sexual assault knows no class or income barriers.

"My God," said one mother upon learning these facts. "What am I supposed to do, tell my children they can't trust *anybody?*"

"No," says Dr. Shulman, "but it's foolish to pretend to children that dangers do not exist. Children are aware of their vulnerability and are naturally concerned about their own safety. It's part of a parent's job to give them the tools to deal with danger realistically. If presented honestly and positively, such information will not threaten children, it will reassure them."

As an important step toward protecting children from sexual assault, parents should consider the confusing "mixed messages" they may be giving about child-adult relationships. Often, for example, parents urge children to submit to physical gestures of affection against their will. Says Pat Fletcher, "Parents see nothing wrong in telling a youngster, 'Go on—give your Aunt Mary a kiss; you haven't seen her in such a long time,' even if the parent *knows* the child detests Aunt Mary. The child who refuses may be criticized for being impolite. This, in effect, says that a child is not entitled to reject an adult whose advances make him or her uncomfortable."

Parents reinforce this idea in a hundred other ways. Such a familiar admonishment as "How can you treat your grandmother that way when you know how much she loves you?" can destroy a child's confidence in his own instincts—yet those instincts are his best defense against adults who would take advantage of him. Remember that sexual abuse of children often begins casually with hugging, kissing and fondling. A simple and determined "No! I don't want you to do that!" can be very effective in discouraging an assailant.

Let's go back to Aunt Mary for a moment. How can a parent handle this situation? If Aunt Mary descends upon little Amanda with the clear intention of smothering her in kisses much to Amanda's distaste, it is appropriate for a parent to side with the child. "Amanda doesn't feel like being kissed today," or "Amanda likes to choose her own times for hugging and kissing," should not offend Aunt Mary too much. Later, Mom or Dad might say to Amanda in private, "I know how you feel about Aunt Mary. It's funny how some hugs and kisses feel wonderful and others feel awful, isn't it?"

This parent would have successfully communicated that the child has the right to make her own decisions about physical intimacy. Such an approach also opens a dialogue on the subject of touching that can be continued later on a level appropriate to the child's age. Within the boundaries of correct social behavior, the parent demonstrates that it's Aunt Mary who lacks manners.

A child's right to personal privacy should also be respected at home if she is to feel comfortable asserting that right elsewhere. But again parents often send mixed signals. For instance, in many households certain areas are "off limits" to kids. But how many children feel confident of preventing intruders from entering a space that is *theirs?* Parents ask children to knock before entering bed- or bathrooms but often forget to give them the same courtesy. No wonder many children think privacy is only for adults.

Children who are used to being respected by adults are the least likely to tolerate adult exploitation. Parents might even consider drawing up a family "Bill of Rights" that specifies areas in which children *and* adults can expect consideration. The right to privacy, the right to say "No!" to harmful or frightening situations, the right to accept only loving and comfortable touches, are taken for granted by most adults. When the same can be said of children, a decline in child sexual assault is likely to follow.

Children also have the right to be informed about dangerous situations and told how to handle them. There's no reason to isolate the issue of sexual assault from other problems discussed at home. The danger of molestation is as real as the danger of fire or getting lost. A "What would you do if . . ." approach can be very effective in opening conversation on these matters; it has a game-like flavor, which appeals to young children, and it allows parents to judge the child's current understanding before presenting information.

"Let's talk about safety," a parent might begin, "and how children can protect themselves in scary situations. For example, what would you do if you and I got separated at the shopping mall and you couldn't find me? If a strange man came to the door when Daddy and I weren't home?" Most children welcome the opportunity to bring their fears on such subjects out in the open and quickly respond by asking "What-if" questions on their own.

"What-if games have taught me a lot about my kids' fears," says one mother who uses this approach regularly with her two preschoolers. "They've also given me the opportunity to correct a lot of misinformation. We often play at mealtimes when everybody is together. Lately my husband and I have begun introducing occasional questions about sexuality and sexual assault. We've asked what they would do if a baby-sitter touched them in a way they didn't like, or if an older friend wanted to undress them and play a secret game that made them feel uncomfortable. We tell them that they should let us know about such things, of course, but we also try to make it clear that their bodies are their possessions—and that they don't have to share them if they don't want to."

The same message can be communicated in other ways, even to children as young as three or four. With preschoolers, for example, a parent might undertake a conversation like this at bedtime:

Parent: Something I really like to do sometimes is tickle your tummy, like this; or hug you, like this; or pretend to eat your ear, like this!

Child: I like that too!

Parent: But if I tickle too hard you can ask me to stop, can't you?

Child: Yes, but I don't want you to stop. Do it again!

Parent: Suppose I was tickling you too hard, and you asked me to stop and I didn't.

Child: That would be mean!

Parent: I think so too. That's why I listen when you say stop. But you know, people *are* mean sometimes. I remember once when I was little, my older brother sat on me and wouldn't let me up no matter how loud I yelled. Can you imagine how I felt?

Child: I bet you were mad.

Parent: I sure was. My feelings were hurt too. It seemed unfair, because he was bigger than I. You know, if anyone ever tries to bully you like that, I hope you'll tell me so we can deal with that person together.

With an older child, a parent might want to be more specific about "touching problems." After reading a book or enjoying some other close activity together, a parent might say:

Parent: It feels good having you near me like this. I wish all touches felt this good. Some kinds of touches are sort of creepy, aren't they?

Child: Yeah, like shaking hands with someone whose hands are clammy.

Parent: Right! Or like getting pushed around in a crowd. How about grown-ups who like to ruffle your hair or pat you on the bottom?

Child: Yuck!

Parent: You know, there are even grown-ups who get a kick out of touching little kids under their clothes.

Child: That's gross!

Parent: I agree, but it's true. I'll tell you a story. When I was little, I had a friend named Betty. Her uncle used to visit her sometimes, and he always liked to have her sit on his lap. Once she was doing that and he started stroking her in a way that made her feel funny. Then he asked if he could put his hand up under her skirt.

Child: What did she do?

Parent: She said she didn't want him to. Her uncle said he would give her a dollar if she'd let him. Betty liked the idea of having a dollar, but she didn't like being close to her uncle that way. So she said no again and went into another room.

Child: That was good.

Parent: Yes, it was. Nobody should have to be touched in a way she doesn't like, don't you agree?

Child: That's right!

Parent: Later my friend told her mother what had happened, and that was a good thing too. Her mother made sure that Betty was never left alone with her uncle again. If anything like that ever happened to you, I hope you'd tell me about it. You can bet I'd be on your side!

This parent has gone beyond warning her child about assault; she has also told the child what to do if an improper advance is ever made. And by declaring her support for the child in advance she has increased the chances that her child will report any incident that occurs. One of the great tragedies of child assault is that many victims feel they can't tell anyone about it—or when they try, they are not believed. This is especially common in cases of incest. Parents sometimes simply cannot accept the idea that a relative could be guilty of such a thing—and children are famous for telling tall tales. Yet experts say children rarely lie about this sort of thing. "*Any* report of sexual abuse should be taken seriously," says Pat Fletcher. "In addition, parents should be on the lookout for sudden changes in behavior that might indicate a problem. If a child becomes unusually withdrawn, has difficulty sleeping or concentrating on schoolwork, or shows an inclination to avoid one member of the family, a warning bell should sound. Parents should try to find out what's wrong."

"What the assaulted child needs most is support," says Dr. Shulman, "and assurance that he or she is not to blame for what has happened. Unfortunately, many children do not get that support. Parents accuse them of fabricating the incident, or even of inviting it. These kids are in for long-term emotional problems on top of whatever physical harm they may have suffered."

What should a parent do when a child reports sexual assault? Above all, say rape counselors, avoid panic. Concentrate on the child and her or his immediate needs. First among these is the need for reassurance that you

- believe what the child has told you,
- understand the child is not at fault,
- are sorry that such an unfortunate thing has happened, and
- will do whatever you can to protect the child in the future.

Other actions can wait until these assurances have been given. Although news that a child has been abused can create overwhelming anger in a parent, it is generally not a good idea to express this to the child. If the offender is someone known, trusted or loved, enraged threats of arrest and jail may make the child feel guilty about telling. "Children who disclose assault incidents aren't looking for revenge," says Suzanne Spier. "They just want it to stop. They want to be told that it's over, that it won't happen again."

Children may or may not want to talk about their experience in detail. Parents can encourage them to express their feelings but shouldn't apply pressure. "I understand that you may not want to talk about this anymore right now, but if it starts bothering you later I hope you'll tell me because I want to try and help" would be an appropriate response. It may not work though. According to Dr. Shulman, some troubled children simply do not feel comfortable talking to their parents—and some parents are too upset to deal with the child effectively. In such cases, an effort should be made to find someone else in whom the child can place his trust.

"Ideally, children should grow up knowing adults other than their parents who care about them and would help them if they need it," Dr. Shulman says. "Parents can say to their kids, 'Look, sometime you may have a problem you don't feel like discussing with me, and I understand that. But there are other people you can turn to.' These might include grandparents or other relatives, ministers, teachers or school counselors. The important thing is for the child to understand that he never has to face a bad situation by himself."

Suzanne Spier adds: "Parents need help too, not only in getting through the immediate crisis, but in dealing with long-term emotional effects. Fortunately, good support services for sexually abused children and their families are being developed in more and more communities as the problem becomes better understood."

Among the decisions to be faced by a parent, once the situation has been emotionally stabilized, is whether or not to report the incident to authorities. If the assailant is a friend or relative, this choice can be truly agonizing. Parents also worry that their children will be further traumatized by encounters with police. If a rape crisis or counseling center is available, it can be a source of sensitive and informed advice on this and other matters—such as the advisability of a medical examination. These organizations know the laws governing child assault (which vary from state to state), can provide victims and their parents with emotional counseling, and are prepared to assist families in dealing with law enforcement agencies. Where rape crisis centers do not exist, help may be available from government agencies concerned with child and family welfare.

"Decisions of this kind should be aimed primarily at protecting the child," says Pat Fletcher. "Sexual assault is a crime, no matter how young the victim or what his or her relationship to the offender. Child assault also usually involves repeated incidents. If you can keep the assailant away from your child, well and good—but he will probably succeed in victimizing someone else. It is also true that it can be very hard to get an offender 'put away,' and the process of arrest and trial can be hard on children. The 'right thing to do' varies from case to case."

One thing is certain: Child sexual assault is a problem nobody wants to face. But we will not put an end to it by pretending it doesn't exist, or by hoping it will go away. We can best protect our children from assault by giving them information about it and making sure that information is truthful. Today that means warning kids about more than being wary of strangers. We must give them the knowledge and the confidence they need to defend themselves, if necessary, from friends.

Turning Away Exploitation

by Susan Newman

Once unmentionable, sexual abuse of children now is in national headlines almost daily. Clearly this problem that has existed for decades is finally being addressed. One study shows a 400 percent increase in sexual abuse reports of children between the years 1977 and 1982. And the age of reported crime victims gets younger every year—more than one-third are children under five. But numbers aside, molestation is out in the open and churning up issues that parents must face and deal with the sooner, the better for their children.

Training your child to recognize an assault and giving him the skills with which to ward off a potential abuse is not an option. It is a parental responsibility as mandatory as providing food, shelter and clothing. And you begin in infancy.

As soon as you start telling your child that "these are your toes, hands, head, fingers," you should be telling her that this is her vagina, his buttocks, his penis, her breasts. "But, we were not taught this way," notes Becky Montgomery, direct services coordinator at Rape and Abuse Crisis Center in Fargo, North Dakota. "Most parents are not comfortable naming and teaching genital terminology to their children."

"That's unfortunate," says Jill Haddad, vice president of the Foundation for America's Sexually Abused Children. "We don't make up strange names for our legs and arms, yet too many parents create nicknames for penises, vaginas and breasts. By calling the private parts of the body by names such as rocket ship, muffin, worm or woo-woo, parents are allowing their children to grow up feeling that there is something wrong with that part of their body."

Susan Newman is the author of *Never Say "Yes" to a Stranger,* a children's book about preventing sexual abuse. "Turning Away Exploitation" is reprinted from *Working Parents,* December/January 1984/85, volume 1, number 6, pp. 23–26. Reprinted by permission of the publisher.

"What adults tend to do with the sexual abuse problem," adds Cordelia Anderson, director of the Sexual Abuse Prevention Program at the Illusion Theatre in Minneapolis, Minnesota (a pioneer in the concept of good, confused and bad touch), "is turn the issue into the 'it' syndrome. We say to children, 'we want you to talk about *it,* if *it* happens you can tell us about *it,* it's not your fault, there's nothing wrong with you if *it* happens.' But we never say what 'it' is."

If a young child is ever to recognize an approaching sexual assault, if he is ever going to be able to tell you what happened, he must know and be able to name the private parts of his body. Explain that his body, especially his private parts, are not to be touched by anyone without his permission.

"Many parents feel that they have to be experts, to have a whole lot of information, before they can begin to talk to their children, but that's not necessary. Just start talking," advises Ms. Anderson. "What you want to do is build on the information your preschooler is already getting."

"Before age three, children learn alot about safety: what hurts, don't play with electric sockets, don't run out in front of cars. We can add to these, personal body safety: no one has the right to touch you in a way that hurts or makes you feel uncomfortable."

You can begin this learning process by asking your preschooler what kinds of touches make him feel good. A hug from grandma? Holding hands with dad? A kiss from sister? Similarly, probe the issue of bad touches to develop the concept in his young mind: "Tell me some touches that you don't think are good ones: An aunt squeezing your cheek? A slap on your back or buttocks? A wet, sloppy kiss?" The point you are trying to make is that bad touching can hurt or give you a creepy feeling. Be specific when you talk with your child: "If someone touches your penis, you should say, 'Don't do that. I don't like it!'"

In order to give young children preventive information they can ultimately use, certain delicate balances in everyday behavior should be maintained. For example, very young children fully understand "no." For most, "no" is far and away the preferred word. While it is important to curtail your child's perpetual use of "no" and to teach her obedience, it is equally important for her to be aware that there are times when she has the right to say "no."

As a parent, respect this right and give your child the opportunity to exercise it. He needs practice to fully comprehend that it's okay to say "no" to an adult in order for him to put the word to use should he ever be approached. Many children fall prey to a child molester simply because they do not realize they can say "no."

"We say the right things: 'your body belongs to you,' but we need to back up what we say," explains Billie Jo Flerchinger, educational coordinator for King County Rape Relief in Renton, Washington.

"Kiss grandpa goodbye. Come on, be a good girl, give your grandpa a kiss. He'll be hurt if you don't." This is a typical farewell scenario between a well-meaning parent and reluctant child. It's also a perfect opportunity to give an otherwise easy-to-manage child the chance to assert herself, to say "no" and have her feelings recognized, not overruled. In situations like this—uncomfortable and difficult for both parent and child—you should support your child. Interfere: say "Shake hands with grandpa instead." Explain to relatives and insistent friends, "we don't want to make Jimmy kiss [hug] anyone if he doesn't want to."

"A child who learns early that he has power, that his parents will back up that power and who has had good information about his body is less susceptible," explains Ms. Flerchinger.

"Make a special effort to encourage questions during these early years," notes Ms. Anderson. "Be patient, try to answer the unending stream of why's, because if you don't, your child will eventually stop asking."

Some important answers are already inside young minds. A child over three understands many of his feelings: happy, sad, hurt, scared. A preschooler may not be able to express all his feelings in words, but he can be taught to trust them—to get away from someone if that person makes them feel "funny" or afraid or wants him to do something he doesn't want to do. But remember, a young child will take this type of self-protective action *only* if he has your permission to say "no" and your encouragement to follow his instincts.

PARENT PRECAUTIONS

In at least 90 percent of child-molesting cases, the abuser is someone the child knows and trusts—a teacher, a close friend, a neighbor, a religious leader, a relative, even a police officer. For this reason don't insist that your child be with someone just because you like the person. If your child is hesitant about staying with a certain babysitter, for instance, or doesn't want to go to school, ask why. Did something upset him?

Molesters look for children who will cooperate and obey, those who are not likely to tell and who aren't assertive. "Children are more often seduced than forced," says Haddad. "These people seduce children by being kind to them; taking them places they want to go and giving them nice things in order to have sex with them." Molesters also tend to victimize children who are more in need of love, affection and attention. However, experts are quick to add that children from loving homes are not immune to sexual exploitation.

During a recent television news interview, convicted pedophile Warren Mumpower told viewers that some parents make it easy to molest children. In this case, he explained that the parents he met were often thrilled to have him interested in the children; glad to have him babysit. But really, shouldn't you question the motives of a 40-year-old man who wants to babysit?

As parents you have to be aware of how teenagers and adults interact with your child. Is someone spending *too* much time with your child, more than a normal parent would spend? Is someone giving him too many gifts? Too often? Taking him to too many places? Is someone giving him an inordinate amount of praise and attention? More than given to other children in the same group?

Consider these issues, too, when investigating care for your preschooler outside your home:

Does the school (center, home) have a good reputation?

Can you drop in anytime? As a parent you have the right to check your child. As one expert on the subject points out, "Preschools and other such facilities will have to adjust to parents dropping in."

Have you observed a class in session? Do the teachers seem to respect the children's feelings and desires? Or do they appear to force the children into activities? Are they patient?

Are you watching your child's response at pick-up time? Is she interacting with other children? Does she genuinely seem to like her caretaker(s)?

"You must learn to trust your own good sense. If something doesn't feel right, take a second look. In most cases, the problem will not be an extreme one, but a change may nevertheless be best for your child," advises Ms. Flerchinger.

At home, don't set up your child for a possible incident by telling him to do whatever the sitter tells him. Explain house rules to your sitter with your child present. Outline bathtime, bedtime and privacy routines. For example, for an older preschooler, "Pam can take her own bath. Please fill the tub for her. She takes her bath with the door closed, by herself." "Johnny can wipe himself after he goes to the bathroom. He doesn't need help." By stating the rules you give your child a sense of control and put the sitter "on notice" that your child is not allowed to keep secrets and that he will tell you if the rules are broken. At the very least, you may short-circuit one of a molester's most powerful tools with children: the secret.

TRAIN YOUR CHILD TO TELL

Children adore secrets. Usually they will keep them, especially if it's an adult who tells them to. Added to that, molesters insure their secrets by imposing horrible—and untrue—consequences if the child tells.

Molesters commonly frighten their innocent victims with such stories as: If you tell, your father or mother will die (or disappear); if you tell, your parents will get a divorce; if you tell, I will say you made me do it; if you tell, no one will be your friend; if you tell, I will never let you stay up late again (or take you to a special place). . . .

It's very easy to sell a threatening secret if a child has no advance information. Essential knowledge such as the difference between a happy secret or surprise and a bad secret can be incorporated into family games and discussions.

"Who Do You Tell?" is a simple game that conditions children to tell when they have a problem and who the proper people are to tell. "Who Do You Tell?" not only teaches self-protection and prevention, but also develops a sense of self-esteem and critical assertiveness. When appropriate to the question, always reassure your child that it's better to tell, that she will not be punished and that it's (if a sexual assault question) never her fault.

"Who Do You Tell?" can be called "What If?" or "Let's Pretend." The thrust and educational value of the questions are the same. Following are some example questions:

- Who do you tell if you lost a mitten at school?
- Who do you tell if your best friend ate all the cookies?
- Who do you tell if your stomach hurts?
- Who do you tell if the babysitter asks you to touch his penis?
- Who do you tell if you think the teacher is not being nice to you?
- Who do you tell if someone knocked you down?
- Who do you tell if someone tells you to keep a secret that isn't a happy secret? (A surprise party or a special gift is a happy secret.)
- Who do you tell if you are spending the night with Aunt Bea or Grandpa Fred and something upsets you?

By rewording your questions, you give a child the chance to get used to saying "no" without being in a real situation:

- What if you are outside playing in front of our house and Mr. Jones invites you into his house to look at the new puppies? (NO, I have to ask my Mom.)
- What if you are walking across the street to pick up Timmy to play and a man you have never seen before starts talking to you? (NO, I can't talk to you. I'm not allowed to talk to strangers.)
- What if someone asks you to cross Locust Avenue and you know you are not allowed to cross that street? (NO, I can't do that.)

EMPOWER YOUR CHILD

The most meaningful way to prevent an unforced seduction is to teach your children what they can do.

"We cannot run around with mass paranoia," writes Jill Haddad in her book, *We Have a Secret.* "If parents will give children permission to tell an adult NO! when that adult wants to touch their body and make them feel uncomfortable and then give them permission to tell, we could stop the molestation of children."

You cannot expect a three-year-old to understand sexual molestation fully, but you can help him cope a little better with sexual advances or orders that confuse and frighten him. Your education should be spontaneous and ongoing with the goal of convincing your child that no one has the right to treat him badly verbally, physically or sexually. Even preschool children can handle this information, if you supply *it*.

Confronting a Near and Present Danger: How to Teach Children to Resist Assault

by Sally Cooper

Twelve-year-old Tanya* and her eight-year-old brother, Marcus, were walking home from school together. Two adolescent boys attacked them and tried to drag Tanya off the sidewalk and into a yard. Without hesitation both kids started shouting a deep guttural self-defense yell while they kicked and fought to get loose. The young attackers ran away.

Tanya and Marcus escaped harm because they had participated in the Child Assault Prevention (CAP) workshops in Columbus, Ohio, the summer before. Though shaken by the attempted assault, they had learned real skills that changed the outcome of a dangerous situation just as clearly as teaching children how to cross the street prevents many pedestrian accidents. Classroom workshops with children in kindergarten through sixth grade have found that children are already very aware of assault situations from television, experience with a school bully, or overhearing adults talking. What they don't know is what to do in such situations. By talking to children in nongraphic, nonviolent language about potential dangers and how to safely maneuver in their world, we replace their fear with confidence, strategies, and real information.

Sally Cooper is co-founder and Executive Director of the National Assault Prevention Center. She is also the founder of the Child Assault Prevention (CAP) Project National Office and co-author of a book about preventing child sexual assault, *Strategies for Free Children.* "Confronting a Near and Present Danger: How to Teach Children to Resist Assault" is reprinted from *Ms. Magazine,* April 1984, pp. 72, 74. Reprinted by permission of the author.
*The children's names are pseudonyms.

In a second-grade class in Upper Arlington, Ohio, a CAP facilitator named Cathy Phelps asks the children if they have the right to eat.

"Of course!" Aisha says.

"How about the right to go to the bathroom?"—Cathy continues.

The children giggle and answer, "Of course."

"What would happen if someone took away your right to eat or go to the bathroom?" With that question the children's expressions change as they imagine that terrible prospect. Cathy then talks about three other important rights: the rights to be "safe, strong, and free," rights that children must be willing to fight for if assault prevention is possible.

In one role-playing exercise a CAP facilitator named Frayda Turkel, pretending to be an older, bigger girl, walks up to her colleague Laurie Kagy and says, "What's in your pocket? You've got lunch money in that pocket, and you are going to give it to me right now."

Confused and frightened, Laurie reaches into her pocket and hands the money to Frayda. "Now you listen to me," says Frayda, grabbing Laurie's arm. "From now on you're going to meet me here every day and give me your lunch money, or else! Do you understand? Don't tell anybody about this either. Now get out of here."

As Laurie and Frayda return to the circle of children, they are smiling and joking to show the class that the pretend scenario is over. Cathy asks the class whether Laurie felt safe, strong, or free in that situation.

"No," volunteers one little girl. "And she'll be hungry today at lunch."

The children discuss strategies to help Laurie: friends will take turns walking her to school to help her resist the bully, to be her witness, and to give her support. They try out various assertive techniques to develop the ability to say no, to stand up for themselves and defend their rights. They learn to think of other children as more than pals to play with, as potential allies. Since so often in assault situations it is another child or a sibling who witnesses the attack, alertness and training for mutual assistance are essential.

Successful prevention techniques begin with a child's ability to identify trouble. Most children tell us that they've been warned about strangers but aren't sure that they would recognize a suspicious one or would know what to do if threatened.

So the second role play involves a stranger who tries to kidnap a boy through trickery. This time a stranger supposedly approaches Frayda, who is playing the part of a boy named Tom. The stranger tells Tom his mother has been hospitalized. The news alarms him. He knows enough not to go immediately with the stranger, but he doesn't know whether to respond by asking for more information, running away, or shouting for help. The children in the classroom learn that a cry for help is their safest recourse. They practice a self-defense yell that is immediately distinguishable from a playful screech in the playground.

Children need a very special yell so that adults know immediately when a child is in danger. They need a yell that makes them feel strong and competent and lets offenders know that they are not going to be passive, easy victims. A friend learned the importance of a self-defense yell one day when her 10-year-old daughter was playing in the garage with a friend. The child's shouts, which my friend believed were part of the play activity, suddenly struck her as much more than just irritating. The mother opened the garage door to find her terrified daughter being molested by a neighbor boy.

Cathy talks about children's right to fight back. "If a man grabs your arm, kick him right in the shin, yelling loud, and run toward a safe location such as a store or a house where people are home. Size or comparable strength doesn't matter if you get him in the shins where everyone is highly sensitive."

The CAP program works as hard at dispelling myths as it does teaching kids to deal with realities. Since 80 percent of all children are assaulted by someone they know and trust, usually a family member, the standard message, "Don't take candy from strangers," will help in a minority of cases.

Another myth is that only female children are victimized. While conservative estimates show that one out of every four girls will be sexually assaulted before 18 years of age, one out of every 11 boys will have a similar experience. To both girls and boys in the class Cathy says slowly and with great intensity, "You have the right not to be touched in ways that frighten, hurt, or confuse you, even if those touches come from someone you know and love." As she describes the next role play, which is aimed at preventing incest, she is careful to acknowledge good touches.

This third role play has Laurie in the part of a child, Frayda pretends to be her Uncle Harry. When Aunt Mary goes shopping, Laurie is left alone in the house with Uncle Harry. He demands that she sit close to him while they're watching television. Laurie complies but looks scared and nervously twists her hair. Then Uncle Harry demands a kiss, bribing Laurie with a promised gift: "How about a 'Smurf' T-shirt? You've always wanted one, haven't you?" When Laurie shyly answers that she'd like the shirt, Uncle Harry uses additional verbal pressure and roughly takes his kiss. We see Laurie frozen in fear just as Aunt Mary returns from the grocery store. Uncle Harry gruffly whispers, "Now you listen to me. I don't want you to tell anybody about this; it will be our little secret."

The adult offender who is known to the child usually doesn't need threats of violence to get compliance. Love, guilt, and fear of adult authority can be coercion enough. Often, the abuser warns children that if they "tell" they will be responsible for sending their daddies to jail, for breaking up the family, or worst of all, that they themselves will be sent to an orphanage or a foster home.

Which "secrets" are not worth protecting is one of the hardest concepts taught by the CAP program. Cathy asks the children to think of a good secret. Robert raises his hand: "A surprise party is a good secret," he says. Amanda volunteers that she knew about her sister's new bike for a whole week before her birthday and never told. Cathy agrees that these are good secrets and explains that good secrets never make us feel scared, guilty, or alone.

"Does Laurie have to keep Uncle Harry's secret if it makes her feel scared or alone?"

A unanimous "no" shakes the classroom.

"So who could Laurie tell?" Cathy asks. Parents, grandparents, a doctor, a caring teacher, a friend's mother, school nurses or counselors are common responses. When Cathy asks if adults always believe what children say happens to them, there is another resounding "no." Because of this credibility problem, she explains how important it is for a child to have at least one trusted adult outside the family to talk to.

The final role-playing exercise is a scene in which Laurie tells Uncle Harry to stop his advances. She says she will tell her mom, Aunt Mary, and her teacher if necessary. When Laurie walks away from Uncle Harry the children in the classroom applaud triumphantly. Cathy, Laurie, and Frayda emphasize again that most incest offenders are scared off by the threat of disclosure and children must exercise that power in order to be safe, strong, and free.

Following the workshop, a child may feel safe enough to ask for immediate help. For instance, Sandra, an eight-year-old in one of our classroom workshops, told us her daddy was "like Uncle Harry. He lies down on top of me and then he bumps up against me hard," she said.

We encouraged Sandra to talk about her secret to the school nurse, who was able to report the trouble to the local children's protective services agency. Sandra approved every step the school took on her behalf because the adults understood how important it was to honor Sandra's great confidence in them.

Children who participate in the decisions that affect their lives will not be further victimized by the process, as happened in another case. A young incest victim confided in her school principal and the next thing she knew two uniformed police officers were outside school asking to talk to her and her father. She told the officers that she had made up the story and then went home to her abuser. The principal had become one more adult in her life who couldn't be trusted.

In order for children to be good decision-makers and problem-solvers we must give them enough information to handle dangerous situations and frequent reassurance that helpless victimization need not be any child's fate. The Child Assault Prevention Project is an effective way to enhance the self-image of children and help them become capable of acting quickly and wisely in a crisis.

The value of the CAP project—and other such prevention projects—lies in its special emphasis on two realities: (1) the danger is not only the stranger in the child's community but is more likely to be a member of the child's own household; (2) coping strategies should focus on autonomy and strength rather than on avoidance and fear.

Women have suffered a great deal from prevention programs that ask them either to rely on men for protection or else to curtail their activities. These options only increase a woman's sense of vulnerability. Children's prevention projects could have the same result unless criteria are built into the programs that recognize these problems. For example, following the early newspaper reports on the killings of Atlanta's children, several articles appeared, which in essence said, "Where were these children's mothers?" Placing the responsibility for social threats on parent's shoulders or reducing children's mobility will only increase children's helplessness. Sound prevention programs will enhance children's own ability to recognize and deal with a potentially dangerous situation.

Sexual Abuse:
Teaching about Touching

by Margo Hittleman

Talking to young people about sexual abuse is difficult for many adults. As parents and educators, we are compelled by concern and awareness of the issue's importance, and yet, at the same time, plagued with doubts. What do we say? How do we say it? Will we be understood? How do we warn children without destroying their ability to trust and share affection spontaneously?

Good books about the prevention of sexual abuse can help by providing the language and format to foster discussions about this difficult subject. With sensitivity and a direct simplicity, they relate their messages in terms that young people can understand in order to provide them with the tools to protect themselves.

The books for the youngest children talk about touching, differentiating between touches that make them feel good (such as hugs from someone we like, petting the dog, sitting in Mommy's lap), touches that make them feel bad (being held too tightly, being tickled too hard, big slurpy kisses), and confusing or secret touches. Touches, they teach, should *never* be secret. Touching that is confusing to the child or games that are labeled a secret should be confided to an adult.

The better books emphasize the right to privacy, teaching that bodies are special. They provide examples of who may touch the child's body and under what circumstances, lending themselves to game-playing with the child about when else it is appropriate for someone to touch their body and when it is not.

Margo Hittleman is a free-lance writer and former information specialist for Cornell University. "Sexual Abuse: Teaching about Touching" is reprinted from *School Library Journal,* January 1985, volume 31, number 5, pp. 34–35. Reprinted by permission of the publisher. The included bibliography was prepared under a grant from the federal government and remains in the public domain.

Most children tend to ignore their own feelings, particularly feelings of discomfort, in deference to adult demands. These books encourage children to recognize their feelings as warnings and to act upon them. Each book presents some version of a simple formula: say no, yell for help, run away, and most importantly, tell someone. Again, they provide a starting point for adult and child to brainstorm situations where one might not feel like touching or being touched and to practice ways to say no.

Books for middle and older elementary school-aged children expand upon these themes. Short stories about children facing potentially exploitive situations with people they know, as in Wachter's *No More Secrets,* can open a discussion about other abusive situations that children might encounter. Children gain a sense of control from knowing how they might handle the unknown. At the same time, they learn that parents want to be told, and, more importantly, that they will be believed.

Books such as Laurie White and Steven Spencer's *Take Care with Yourself* talk about feelings and place their emphasis on developing the child's sense of self-worth. Two other books in this category, *Liking Myself* (for younger children) and *The Mouse, the Monster, and Me!* (for ages 8 and up), also merit note. While they do not specifically address sexual abuse, their focus on self-worth and assertiveness make them useful prevention aids.

Adolescents who have themselves been abused are drawn to fiction portraying others in similar situations, such as Toni Morrison's *The Bluest Eye.* Unfortunately, young adult fiction is still limited, especially in terms of young male victims of sexual abuse. However, older adolescents will find Katherine Brady's *Father's Day* and Charlotte Allen's *Daddy's Girl* accessible. Although not written specifically for a young adult audience, many sexually abused adolescents identify with the stories of the authors' incestuous childhoods. Presenting adult perspectives, they indicate that it is possible to grow up and lead a normal life.

In general, the better books for young people tackle their subjects directly. Books that are vague or hint at "bad things" that people may do are confusing and frightening to children and offer no protection. Similarly, books emphasizing only potential dangers from strangers don't equip young people to deal with what is more likely to happen—exploitation by adults they know and trust. Stories should be racially mixed and avoid an overly sterotyped nuclear family image. Finally, books should address young people's power to protect themselves and to accomplish a positive resolution of exploitative incidents.

Guides for parents are welcome complements to the books for young people. Protection only begins with a "read aloud" story. Prevention of child sexual abuse requires continued parental support. These books address the discomfort that often accompanies talking with children about sexual issues and offer practical strategies for teaching young people safety skills. They also provide information for the parents who learn that their child has been abused. Librarians can provide additional assistance by creating displays and developing lists of local resources.

As awareness of child sexual abuse increases, the need to provide young people with the skills to prevent victimization becomes more apparent. Librarians can help by providing parents with the tools to lay the foundations for safety.

FOR PRESCHOOL AND ELEMENTARY SCHOOL

Dayee, Frances S. *Private Zone: a Book Teaching Children Sexual Assault Prevention Tools.* Warner Bks. 1982. $2.95. PreS-Gr 1
Emphasizing the concept of privacy, Dayee discusses who may touch the child's body and under what circumstances. Included is information for parents about sexual assault.

Freeman, Lory. *It's My Body.* Parenting Pr. (7750 31st Ave., NE, Suite 404-A. Seattle, Wash. 98115) no date. $7.95. PreS-Gr 4
Different situations help children distinguish between appropriate and inappropriate touching and how to respond. (A parents' resource guide is also available.)

Hindman, Jan. *A Very Touching Book.* McClure-Hindman Bks. (P.O. Box 208, Durkee, Oreg. 97905) 1983. $7.95. Gr 3 Up
With humorous, colorful illustrations, this book discusses good, bad, and secret touching. It teaches children the proper names for genitalia and emphasizes that children have the right to say no to sexual touching.

Montgomery, Becky & others. *Annie: Once I Was a Little Bit Frightened.* Rape and Abuse Crisis Center. (P.O. Box 1655, Fargo, N. Dak. 58107) 1983. $1.50 plus postage. PreS-Gr 4
The story of Annie, a victim of a neighbor's touching, helps to elicit information about abuse that may have already occurred.

Palmer, Pat. *Liking Myself.* Impact Publishers. (P.O. Box 1094, San Luis Obispo, Calif. 93406) 1977. $3.95. PreS-Gr 4
An introduction to the concepts of feelings, self-esteem, and assertiveness.

Palmer, Pat. *The Mouse, the Monster, and Me!* Impact Publishers. (P.O. Box 1094, San Luis Obispo, Calif. 93406) 1977. Gr 3 Up
Non-assertive "mice" and aggressive "monsters" help young people to develop a sense of personal rights and responsibilities and to become appropriately assertive.

Wachter, Oralee. *No More Secrets for Me.* Little. 1984. $12.95. Gr 3 Up
Four stories about children facing exploitive situations. The book emphasizes the child's right to say "no" and encourages confiding in a trusted adult.

White, Laurie & Steven Spencer. *Take Care with Yourself: a Young Person's Guide to Understanding, Preventing and Healing from the Hurts of Child Abuse.* Take Care With Yourself. (915 Maxine Ave., Flint, Mich. 48503) 1983. $5.95. Gr 3 Up
Addressing feelings and concepts of self-worth, this book explains how and why people hurt other people, emphasizes that no one deserves to be hurt, and lets young people know where to find help.

Williams, Joy. *Red Flag, Green Flag People.* rev. ed. Rape and Abuse Crisis Center. (P.O. Box 1655, Fargo, N. Dak. 58107) 1983. $3. plus postage. PreS-Gr 2
This coloring book discusses different types of touching and teaches children to say no, to run away, and to tell an adult.

FOR YOUNG ADULTS

Allen, Charlotte Vale. *Daddy's Girl.* Wyndham/S. & S. 1980. $10.95; Berkley 1982. pap $2.95. Gr 9 Up

Brady, Katherine. *Father's Days: a True Story of Incest.* Dell. 1981. $2.95. Gr 9 Up
Allen's and Brady's books are fictionalized accounts of their incestuous childhoods.

Hyde, Margaret O. *Sexual Abuse: Let's Talk About It.* Westminster. 1984. $8.95. Gr 5 Up
A book to help children understand what sexual abuse is, what to do if it happens, why they should not feel guilty, where to go for help, and what will happen when they seek it.

Morrison, Toni. *The Bluest Eye.* Washington Square Pr. 1970. $2.95. Gr 7 Up
Pecola, an 11-year-old black girl, prays nightly for blue eyes so that she will be beautiful and noticed. She is finally noticed—by her alcoholic father, who rapes her.

Swan, Helen & Gene Mackey. *Dear Elizabeth: The Diary of an Adolescent Victim of Sexual Abuse.* Children's Institute of Kansas City. (9412 High Drive, Leawood, Kans. 66206) 1984. $4.95. Gr 6-12
Brenda attempts to deal with her father's molestation of her in this fictional account that typifies many aspects of incest.

Top Secret: Sexual Assault Information for Teenagers Only. King County Rape Relief. (Dept. DM, 305 S. 43rd St., Renton, Wash. 98055) 1982. $4. Gr 7 Up
A booklet that answers questions about incest and rape, with an emphasis on self-protection.

FOR PARENTS

Adams, Caren & Jennifer Fay. *No More Secrets: Protecting Your Child from Sexual Assault.* Impact Publishers (P.O. Box 1094, San Luis Obispo, Calif. 93406) 1981. $3.95.
Ways to talk with children about sexual abuse. Adams suggests games to teach preventional skills, lists indications of possible abuse, tells what to do if an assault has occurred, and gives suggestions for dealing with the crisis.

HE TOLD ME Not to Tell! King County Rape Relief. (305 S. 43rd St., Renton, Wash. 98055) 1979. $2.50.
All of the information from Adams' *No More Secrets* is covered here in a much briefer, more direct form.

Sanford, Linda T. *The Silent Children: a Book for Parents About Prevention of Child Sexual Abuse.* McGraw-Hill. 1982. $7.95.
Information and activities to help parents help children to protect themselves from sexual assault. The second section contains essays on this topic.

Sanford, Linda T. *Come Tell Me Right Away: a Positive Approach to Warning Children About Sexual Abuse.* Linda Sanford. (123 Sutherland Rd., Brookline, Mass. 02146) no date. $1.75.
A 24-page summary of *The Silent Children.*

Child Sexual Abuse Prevention: Tips to Parents

by U.S. Department of Health and Human Services,
Office of Human Development Services,
Administration for Children, Youth and Families,
National Center on Child Abuse and Neglect

LISTEN AND TALK WITH YOUR CHILDREN

Perhaps the most critical child sexual prevention strategy for parents is good communication with your children. This is not only challenging to every parent but also can be difficult, especially for working parents and parents of adolescents.

- Talk to your child every day and take time to really listen and observe. Learn as many details as you can about your child's activities and feelings. Encourage him or her to share concerns and problems with you.
- Explain that his or her body belongs only to them alone and that he or she has the right to say no to anyone who might try to touch them.
- Tell your child that some adults may try to hurt children and make them do things the child doesn't feel comfortable doing. Often these grownups call what they're doing a secret between themselves and the child.
- Explain that some adults may even threaten children by saying that their parents may be hurt or killed if the child ever shares the secret. Emphasize that an adult who does something like this is doing something that is wrong.

"Child Sexual Abuse Prevention: Tips to Parents" was published by the U.S. Department of Health and Human Services, Office of Human Development Services, Administration for Children, Youth and Families, and the National Center on Child Abuse and Neglect. The following statement appears on the publication: "We encourage photocopying or reprinting this information."

- Tell your child that adults whom they know, trust and love or someone who might be in a position of authority (like a babysitter, an uncle, a teacher or even a policeman) might try to do something like this. Try not to scare your children—emphasize that the vast majority of grownups never do this and that most adults are deeply concerned about protecting children from harm.
- Make sure that your child knows that if someone does something confusing to them, like touching or taking a naked picture or giving them gifts, that you want to be told about it. Reassure the child and explain that he or she will not be blamed for whatever an adult does with the child.

OBSERVE PHYSICAL AND BEHAVIORAL SIGNS

Children who may be too frightened to talk about sexual molestation may exhibit a variety of physical and behavioral signals. Any or several of these signs may be significant. Parents should assume responsibility for noticing such symptoms including:

- Extreme changes in behavior such as loss of appetite.
- Recurrent nightmares or disturbed sleep patterns and fear of the dark.
- Regression to more infantile behavior such as bedwetting, thumb sucking, or excessive crying.
- Torn or stained underclothing.
- Vaginal or rectal bleeding, pain, itching, swollen genitals, and vaginal discharge.
- Vaginal infections or venereal disease.
- Unusual interest in or knowledge of sexual matters, expressing affection in ways inappropriate for a child of that age.
- Fear of a person or an intense dislike at being left somewhere or with someone.
- Other behavioral signals such as aggressive or disruptive behavior, withdrawal, running away or delinquent behavior, failing in school.

CHOOSING A PRESCHOOL OR CHILD CARE CENTER

Although the vast majority of this nation's preschools and child care centers are perfectly safe places, recent reports of child sexual abuse in these settings are a source of great concern to parents.

- Check to make sure that the program is reputable. State or local licensing agencies, child care information and referral services, and other child care community agencies may be helpful sources of information. Find out whether there have been any past complaints.

- Find out as much as you can about the teachers and caregivers. Talk with other parents who have used the program.
- Learn about the school or center's hiring policies and practices. Ask how the organization recruits and selects staff. Find out whether they examine references, background checks, and previous employment history before hiring decisions are made.
- Ask whether and how parents are involved during the day. Learn whether the center or school welcomes and supports participation. Be sensitive to the attitude and degree of openness about parental participation.
- Ensure that you have the right to drop in and visit the program at any time.
- Make sure you are informed about every planned outing. Never give the organization blanket permission to take your child off the premises.
- Prohibit in writing the release of your child to anyone without your explicit authorization. Make sure that the program knows who will pick up your child on any given day.

IF YOU THINK THAT YOUR CHILD HAS BEEN ABUSED . . .

- Believe the child. Children rarely lie about sexual abuse.
- Commend the child for telling you about the experience.
- Convey your support for the child. A child's greatest fear is that he or she is at fault and responsible for the incident. Alleviating this self-blame is of paramount importance.
- Temper your own reaction, recognizing that your perspective and acceptance are critical signals to the child. Your greatest challenge may be to not convey your own horror about the abuse.
- Do not go to the school or program to talk about your concern. Instead, report the suspected molestation to a social services agency or the police.
- Find a specialized agency that evaluates sexual abuse victims— a hospital or a child welfare agency or a community mental health therapy group. Keep asking until you find a group or an individual with appropriate expertise.
- Search for a physician with the experience and training to detect and recognize sexual abuse when you seek a special medical examination for your child. Community sexual abuse

treatment programs, childrens' hospitals and medical societies may be sources for referrals.

- Talk with other parents to ascertain whether there are unusual behavior or physical symptoms in their children.
- Remember that taking action is critical because if nothing is done, other children will continue to be at risk. Child sexual abuse is a community interest and concern.

Finally, do not blame yourself. Sexual abuse is a fact in our society. Many individuals who molest children find work through employment and community activities which give them access to children. The vast majority of abuse occurs in situations where the child knows and trusts the adult. Do your homework well, but remember a community and national consciousness is needed before we can stamp out sexual molestation in our society.

SECTION III

The Sexually Abused Child: Identification and Treatment

Introduction

Sexual abuse is an onerous crime against children. The offensive nature of the act, combined with the enormity of its implications, create an aura of unbelievability which the victims often have to combat. It is our society's responsibility to dispel the myths and mistrust that surround this crime, and this section is an effort in that direction. It begins with "Is the Child Victim of Sexual Abuse Telling the Truth?" by Dr. Kathleen Coulborn Faller. This article examines the motivation of those involved in sexual abuse cases and clearly delineates what indications an evaluator should look for when gathering data to substantiate abuse.

Though a high percentage of the reported victims in cases of sexual abuse are female, being male does not offer protection from this crime. Maria Nasjleti, in her article "Suffering in Silence: The Male Incest Victim," discusses the particular problems of being a male incest victim and proposes reasons why these cases of abuse go unreported.

Dr. Christine Adams-Tucker's report on the victim's psychological damage concludes this section. "Defense Mechanisms Used by Sexually Abused Children" exposes the reader to the pathological results that may occur following the sexual victimization of a child.

Is the Child Victim of Sexual Abuse Telling the Truth?

by Kathleen Coulborn Faller

INTRODUCTION

Often in cases of sexual abuse child welfare workers and mental health experts are asked whether or not a child's allegation of sexual mistreatment can be taken at face value or believed. If the child's story is trusted, the implications for action are far-reaching for both the child and the family. On the other hand, if the child is not believed and the allegation is true, the effect on the child will almost surely be devastating. Clearly, mental health professionals need guidance in assessing children's allegation of sexual mistreatment. The purpose of this article is to provide such guidance.

This article addresses two facets of the investigation: the motives the various actors in sexually abusive situations have for being truthful or lying and a procedure for assessing an allegation of sexual abuse. It is necessary for the professional to understand not only the steps which need to be taken in an evaluation but also the family or interpersonal context of sexual abuse.

The article's main concern will be sexual abuse where there are female victims and male perpetrators (this configuration represents 75–90% of reported cases [1, 2]) and on incestuous situations. Further, it will be especially concerned with the problem of substantiating sexual abuse of young children.

In this article incest is the term used for cases where there is a blood relationship between the victim and perpetrator. Sexual assault is the term for cases when victim and perpetrator are not blood

Kathleen Coulborn Faller is Assistant Professor, School of Social Work, and Co-director of the University of Michigan Inter-Disciplinary Project on Child Abuse and Neglect. "Is the Child Victim of Sexual Abuse Telling the Truth?" is reprinted by permission of the author and publisher from *Child Abuse and Neglect,* 1984, volume 8, pp. 473–481. Copyright © 1984, Pergamon Press.

relatives. The perpetrator in assault might be a stranger, a friend of the family, or the mother's boyfriend.

WHO HAS THE MOST TO LOSE?

The Victim

The evaluator needs to approach an allegation of sexual abuse with a clear understanding of who has a vested interest in lying and who in telling the truth. The victim places herself in considerable jeopardy as a result of telling the truth. She may be rejected by the perpetrator and ostracised by her family. She may be "punished" by placement in foster care or an institution. Her family may be torn apart, and she may see herself as responsible for its demise. She will have to tell the intimate details of her story to many people. Both the shame and guilt for having been involved in the sexual abuse, and the feeling of being responsible for any negative consequences to the family may inhibit her from telling. If the case goes to court, she may have to describe the intimate details of the abuse to strangers with the perpetrator facing her, and she may be subjected to harsh cross-examination by the perpetrator's attorney.

Frequently the perpetrator will threaten the victim with some of these consequences and urge her not to tell. Children in such a situation feel helpless in the face of a powerful adult. Because of the anticipated consequences, victims may keep the secret for months and sometimes years [3, 4]. Delay in the report of sexual abuse, therefore, is to be expected and ought not to be seen as a reason to question the veracity of the allegation. It is especially likely when there is a close personal relationship between the victim and the perpetrator. Nor is it uncommon for a child to reveal that she has been sexually abused, and then retract her story as she experiences the negative consequences of telling for herself and her family [5].

The Perpetrator

For his part, the perpetrator has everything to lose if the child's story is believed, and thus, in most cases, will deny he has sexually abused the child when indeed he has. He will likely face rejection by the immediate family and the extended family as well. Especially in father-daughter incest cases, divorce may ensue. In some instances, his employment may be in jeopardy. If the abuse is incest, he has reason to fear the juvenile court which may deprive him of his child, impose treatment, and intrude in other ways into the family. The perpetrator has even more cause to fear the criminal court, where he may be tried for criminal sexual conduct and sent to prison, or at least placed on probation.

In addition to the practical consequences of admission are the psychological ones. Many perpetrators are so ashamed of their behavior that they cannot admit it. For some the shame is so great they will continue to deny in the face of overwhelming evidence. Furthermore, a substantial percentage of sexual abusers are to some extent character disordered; these men may lie, and lie convincingly and persistently over a period of months and even years. In their endeavor to persuade the decision maker of their innocence, they may enlist the help of family and friends.

Mothers

Mothers may also have a lot to lose if the victim's allegation is believed, particularly in father-daughter incest cases. First, to acknowledge the incest exists may be regarded by the mother as an indictment of her as a mother and a spouse. This may be so painful that "putting on blinders" is a more tolerable solution. Moreover, sexual abuse often develops when there are deficiencies in the sexual relationship between perpetrator (spouse or boyfriend) and mother. She may not want a sexual relationship with the perpetrator. Usually unconsciously, but sometimes consciously, she may facilitate the movement of the daughter into the incestuous relationship. Thus, even though she may not recognize them, there may be costs for the mother if the sexual abuse ends [6, 7].

The mother may also be facing more concrete and practical problems, for instance, financial dependency on the perpetrator. If she has to expel him, or if he goes to prison, she may have to seek other means of support. This can include going on Aid for Families with Dependent Children (AFDC), or seeking employment when she has never worked or has not worked in years.

Finally, should her spouse leave or be incarcerated, she will lose the emotional support he may have provided. To an outsider this may not seem much, but frequently he will be all the mother has, and she will not be able to imagine life without him. Many mothers of incest victims suffer from low self-esteem, and are very dependent upon their partners. They may choose their partners over their children if forced to choose one or the other.

Because of these dynamics, mothers of sex abuse victims often do not believe their daughters' allegations, ignore them when they are made, or try to deal with the problem without bringing in outside help. Alternatively, they may initially side with the child, but then switch their loyalties, and side with the perpetrator as they experience the practical consequences of the spouse's anger and/or loss of the spouse.

EXAMINING THE CHILD'S STORY

For the reasons stated above, we know that children do not make up stories asserting they have been sexually molested. It is not in their interests to do so. Young children do not have the sexual knowledge necessary to fabricate an allegation. Clinicians and researchers in the field of sexual abuse are in agreement that false allegations by children are extremely rare [7]. Further in those unusual instances where they do occur, there is usually some serious malfunction in the family.

In the past, some mental health professionals attributed children's allegations of incest to oedipal fantasies. Not only may it be easier to believe these assertions are fantasies than the truth, but there is support from Freud's writings and the psychoanalytic literature for this position [8, 9]. Freud concluded when faced with accounts of incest by women diagnosed as hysterical that these recollections were fantasies [10]. Today many professionals believe that Freud was wrong in assuming categorically such allegations were fantasies [11, 12]. Moreover it is relatively easy to differentiate what is currently regarded as an oedipal fantasy from a report of sexual abuse.

Generally children preoccupied with oedipal fantasies will be between the ages of 3 and 6, or the recollection itself is from that time in the child's life. The content of an oedipal fantasy consists of ideas of getting close to and being loved by the desired parent and excluding the other parent, rather than of any explicitly sexual material [13, 14]. For example, a 4-year-old girl asserted she was going to marry someone named "Raddy," whom she said looked like her daddy when he was 5, and they were going to go to California so Raddy's mother would not be able to live with them.

Reports of sexual abuse can be differentiated from such fantasies by the victim's ability to give very specific details about what took place, assuming she is willing to discuss the incident(s). This includes details about the sexual abuse and surrounding events. In cases where the child is verbal, the best way to gather information is to ask about the last time the sexual abuse happened. Considerable detail can usually be elicited at least about the surrounding events, making the idiosyncratic nature of the incident quite clear. For example, a 6-year-old girl reported, "It was raining and I thought my daddy was asleep so I was playing in my brother's room where I'm not supposed to play. My daddy came in and I thought he would be mad at me, but he said he wouldn't be mad if I laid on the bed with him." The scenario related here is quite unique. Probes should be used if such detail is not automatically forthcoming. For instance, the interviewer might ask the victim what she was wearing, who else was at home, or what time of the day it was.

The child may be much more reticent about giving details of the sexual abuse than about recounting events surrounding the incident and this detail may require probing. To assure the veracity of the child's assertions, the interviewer should be looking for specific detail about the sexual behavior, a description which seems told from a child's viewpoint, and an emotional response consistent with the nature of the sexual abuse. For example, a 3½-year-old described her stepfather's digital penetration during self-masturbation as follows: "First he undressed me, then himself. He put two fingers in me, one in the front and said he was making white sugar and one in the back and said he was making brown sugar. He rubbed his bottom when he did it." When asked whether he rubbed himself in the front or back, she pointed to the penis on an anatomically explicit doll. While relating this story, she was visibly upset. When she was finished, she said it was "gross" and it hurt.

Prior to discussing the sexual events, the interviewer needs to find out what names the child uses for private parts, and then use them in the questioning. This can be done by asking a trusted adult, or the child if no adult is available. If the child does not provide detail of sexual abuse spontaneously, sometimes it can be elicited by asking such questions as, "Did he touch your privates?" "Did he put his finger inside?" A less preferable alternative is for the evaluator to relate what she/he thinks happened and ask the child to respond "Yes" or "No" to each statement. It is desirable, however, to get a spontaneous statement of the events in order to avoid a situation where the evaluator might be putting words into the child's mouth. This is particularly important if the case is going to court.

A young child may be somewhat confused about the exact sequence of events, or may forget parts of the story at times, but these discrepancies should not call into question the veracity of the story. Further, young children may not be able to affix dates or exact times to incidents of abuse. However, they will usually be able to locate such acts in relation to significant events in their lives (e.g., on my birthday, the day it snowed, the nights when mommy goes out bowling, about supper time).

In gathering data about sexual abuse, the interviewer should try to find out whether the abuse hurt, "felt funny" or "felt good." Information should be gathered about what, if anything, the perpetrator said to the child about the sexual abuse: Was she threatened or told not to tell or bribed? The interviewer should probe for information about incidents of sexual abuse other than the most recent one by asking whether any abuse happened before the incident already described, and if so, how often and what took place. The victim should be asked if she knows whether the perpetrator ever did this kind of thing with anyone else. Thus, the goal of the interviewer is not only to elicit specific detail from the victim, but to also get a broader picture of the perpetrator's sexual activity with children. In incest cases, the interviewer should expect a history of sexual abuse over time, if the child is old enough. In contrast, cases of sexual assault are more likely to be single sexual encounters or intermittent ones.

STRATEGIES FOR CORROBORATING THE CHILD'S STORY

The Child's Statement to Significant Others

Sometimes knowledge about a sexual abuse incident is based solely upon physical evidence. However, more often cases of sexual abuse come to professional attention because the child has made a statement to someone, other than the evaluator, about the molestation. (In such a case there may be or may not be physical evidence.) The interviewer should talk directly with those persons to get all the information they have, and to assess the reliability of these reports.

Often a child will be candid with a parent or relative, but will be quite reticent with a professional. If this problem is anticipated, it may be possible to have those persons whom the child has told tape record the child's statements at home where the child feels less threatened. It is also a good practice to have such a person present during the interview, but some time will be needed alone with the child. In certain instances a child may feel less free to talk with a trusted adult because she does not want to upset that person, or because she does not want to make that person angry at the perpetrator.

In some cases children will refuse to talk during an evaluation, but later they will talk about the incident. Caretakers should be instructed that if this happens, they should tape record or write down the child's statements or telephone the evaluator and have the child repeat assertions over the phone. The professional should also tell the caretaker to take note of anything the child does subsequently which appears to be related to the abuse. For example, two sisters, ages 3 and 5, who had been sexually abused by their father, repeatedly simulated intercourse with one another after the evaluation. The 5-year-old had a bad dream in which she said, "My daddy pooped in my mouth." One type of sexual abuse in this case was fellatio.

Using the Media of Play, Pictures, or Stories

Certain behaviors and patterns which can be elicited in doll play, drawing, story telling, and other projective techniques, may be invaluable in corroborating an allegation of sexual abuse. With children who are reluctant to talk, information gathered in an indirect manner may be the only data that can be elicited in a formal evaluation. Depending upon the child's level of comfort, the evaluator may want to precede any direct questioning with attempts to elicit sexual content in play. Using these media to gather information is also less threatening to the child than direct questioning. The interviewer must be patient, and willing to spend two or three hours and sometimes several sessions gathering information.

What one looks for are sexual themes or content in the child's play, pictures, or stories. A useful process is as follows: The interviewer initially allows the child to use the medium in whatever way she wants. Sexual content may surface spontaneously. Whether it does or not, the evaluator will eventually want to structure the interaction so it focuses on the context in which the sexual abuse is thought to have taken place. For example, if a doll house and doll play are used, the interviewer will begin by allowing the child to play with the dolls in the doll house. Sexual concerns might emerge right away. The child may undress all the dolls and look between their legs or make the dolls engage in sexual acts. The worker will nevertheless want to structure the situation by focusing, for example, on a daddy doll and a little girl doll and ask, "What do daddies and little girls do together?" or "What does the daddy doll do with the little girl doll?" The child might then put the two dolls to bed together, one on top of the other. Such a pattern is likely to be repeated in various configurations. It is important then to ask whether the child engages in this behavior with her daddy, or ask what she does with her own daddy. A potential disadvantage of indirect methods of assessment is that the evaluator may elicit sexual themes in play but may not be able to tie these to the sexual abuse. By maneuvering the play context closer to the actual allegation, it is possible to make the link between general sexual content and the reported sexual abuse. This technique is particularly useful with young children whose language is limited. In such cases, the evaluator can rely on a combination of showing and telling.

Similar strategies can be employed with picture drawing and story telling. Picture drawing is appropriate for children of about 4 to 10. A 5-year-old evaluated by the author was asked to draw a picture of "anything." She drew a picture of her father with a penis, or as she said, "The peanuts." She was then asked to tell about "the peanuts," what it does and when she might have seen it. She then spoke of her father "trying to get bugs and maggots out of her vaginita (vagina) with his fingers while rubbing his peanuts against her butt." Making up stories in response to projective pictures is useful with children a little older. Sometimes a fruitful technique is to ask a child to draw a picture and then tell a story about it.

Anatomically explicit dolls can be useful aids in the assessment process. However, because most children have not had previous exposure to such dolls, they will elicit some unusual responses. Laughter, expressions of mild distaste, pulling on the private parts, and making the dolls go "potty" are normal reactions. Fear, anxiety, and vehement denial of knowledge about private parts are more worrisome patterns, and may be clues to sexual abuse.

In addition unstructured play with these dolls may elicit explicit sexual interactions from sexually abused children, while nonvictims might persist in having the dolls go "poop and pee." For example, one victim evaluated by the author put the daddy doll's penis in her mouth three times. This pattern was interspersed with fighting behavior between the mommy and daddy doll. A 9-year-old mildly retarded girl reenacted several times a scenario where a brother and sister were downstairs watching television. They then "smooched" repeatedly. Smooching involved sexual intercourse and concurrent kissing. She had been sexually abused by her 16-year-old brother over several years. As with doll house play, the interviewer can restructure the play context progressively closer to the alleged incident(s) of sexual abuse.

However, anatomically explicit dolls have additional utility. Because of their explicit nature, children can show what happened with the dolls rather than having to talk about it. They can do this by reenacting the scene of the sexual abuse. Alternatively, they can point to parts of the girl doll where they may have been touched, kissed, or penetrated, or to parts of the daddy doll they were induced to fondle or kiss, or which were put inside them.

We must also understand why certain children are not forthcoming about molestation, and, therefore, why indirect methods are necessary. First, the interviewer is likely to be relatively unknown to the child and usually less well known than the perpetrator. Children may admit the abuse to someone they trust—mother, an aunt, or a friend of the family—but be much less willing to make the revelation to a stranger. A related point is that in many cases even though the child has been molested by the perpetrator, the child may be attached to him, and will not want to cause him trouble. Alternatively, as noted earlier, the child may fear negative consequences for the family, or retribution by the perpetrator if she reveals the sexual abuse.

The Child's Knowledge of Sexual Matters

Another important part of substantiating a sexual abuse allegation may be assessing the child's sexual knowledge. The data may be gathered in an interview, or by using information from other sources. Children who have been victims often are far more aware of sexual matters than most children of their age, or they may possess sexual information for which the family cannot explain a source. For example, a child of 4 who has been sexually abused may know a penis gets big and white juice comes out of it. In a recent evaluation, the author, using anatomically explicit dolls, asked a 3-year-old what daddies do with their "dinkies," (the child's word for penis). She replied, "Girls kiss it." While children may gain such knowledge from observation of sexual acts, it is not likely. If observation is the source of the victim's information, there is still cause to be concerned.

Sexual Behavior

Sexual behavior on the part of the child is another source of corroborative data. This is different from specific information elicited through play or questioning in an interview. It is generally more spontaneous and may occur in the context of the interview or in other settings. These sexual behaviors will vary with the age of the child. Generally, such evidence is more likely to be observed in younger children.

Excessive masturbation is one kind of behavior to look for in young children. While all children masturbate, molested children may do so to a marked degree. They may masturbate when they are upset, when they are questioned about the sexual abuse, or when they need comfort. They do so even though they are told not to. Some will injure their genitals in the course of repeated masturbation.

Young children who have been sexually molested may also initiate sexual encounters with others. In a day-care or hospital setting, they may sexually accost other children. In such a context, they may take on the role of the aggressor and victimize other children, or they may persist in their victim role. Sexually abused children may also attempt to elicit sexual responses from adults for whom they have some affection. We think they assume sexual interaction is the way adults and children who like one another show affection. Thus, a little girl may rub a male worker's penis, or wiggle her bottom on his lap. A boy who has been a victim of a female perpetrator may attempt to squeeze a nurse's breasts [15].

Latency-aged victims are often described as seductive and extremely concerned with their physical appearance. They may appear unusually feminine and coy. It is important for professionals to understand that victims have been socialized by perpetrators into a seductive pattern. Thus, whatever active role they play is a consequence of this socialization process. As these children grow older and reach early adolescence, they may become quite sexually active and be described as promiscuous. The sexual encounters may be with peers or with older men. To illustrate, the mother of a 12-year-old girl complained that her daughter was very promiscuous, to the point that she had contracted gonorrhea three times. An evaluation uncovered that this child's promiscuity was preceded by sexual abuse by her father and stepfather. Some victims will also engage in prostitution as adolescents or as adults [16].

Other Behavioral Indicators

Additional supportive evidence is behavior which suggests a child's anxiety or troubled mental state. Behavioral symptoms stemming from this can be the result of sexual abuse.

With young children regression is frequently seen with the onset of sexual abuse. A child who previously was toilet trained may begin to wet the bed. A child who was easy to put to bed may become fearful of the dark, and refuse to go to bed without a trusted adult in the room. Nightmaring and nightwalking may also occur. For example, a 6-year-old evaluated by the author insisted on taking her "blankie" to school and had nightmares and wet the bed as a result of sexual abuse by her father.

A child's fear of the perpetrator may generalize to all men (assuming the perpetrator is a man). Sometimes this fear is more apparent with other men than with the perpetrator. Children also may appear depressed and become withdrawn. Victims who previously did well in school sometimes present with school problems. Often observers note a personality change in the victim which seems to coincide with the onset of the abuse. Thus, one victim's mother stated her daughter was "a motor mouth" before the molestation began, but now appears to be withdrawn and worried. In many cases, such symptoms as just described, occur after the abuse incident, diminish, and recur when another act of sexual abuse takes place.

Adolescents may present with acting out or self-destructive behavior. Thus, the adolescent victim may run away, be truant from school, be involved in fights and other aggression, have very hostile relations with her parents, often worse with mother than the father, steal and shoplift, and in general appear out of control. As a rule, the intensity of the adolescent victim's acting out is greater than the typical adolescent rebellion. Professionals may suggest institutional treatment for these victims because their deviance is so severe, frequently without comprehending the underlying cause. Self-destructive patterns found in adolescent victims are alcoholism, drug use and addiction, self-mutilation, and attempts at suicide, as well as successful suicides.

CONCLUSION

In order to evaluate an allegation of sexual abuse objectively, professionals must both be aware of the propensity of the different parties in the case to lie and have a grasp of how to go about assessing an allegation. If the evaluator takes a child's statements which may have been forthcoming in a formal interview, made to significant others but not to the professional, or made at one point and later retracted, and buttresses these with other information, a clear picture will evolve. Supplementary data may include sexual content in the child's play, picture drawing or story telling, sexual behavior on the part of the child, sexual knowledge beyond that expected for the child's age, and nonsexual behavioral indicators that the child is under stress. Obviously, the more supportive data the evaluator has, the more convinced he/she will be, and the more persuasive the evaluator's report will be to others. However, the only information which should not be taken by itself as a sign there has been sexual abuse is the nonsexual behavioral indicators. Those indicators can also be a result of problems other than sexual ones.

REFERENCES

1. Herman, J. and Hirschman, L. Father-daughter incest. In: *The Sexual Victimology of Youth,* L.C. Schultz (Ed.), p. 98. Charles C. Thomas, Springfield, IL (1980).

2. Kempe, C.H. Sexual abuse: Another hidden pediatric problem. *Pediatrics* **62:**382–389 (1978).

3. Herman, J. and Hirschman, L. Lisa. In: *The Sexual Victimology of Youth,* L.C. Schultz (Ed.), p. 109. Charles C. Thomas, Springfield, IL (1980).

4. Rush, F. *The Best Kept Secret: Sexual Abuse of Children.* Prentice Hall, Englewood Cliffs, NJ (1980).

5. Zaphiris, A. *Incest: The Family with Two Known Victims.* American Humane Association, Englewood, CO (1978).

6. Jiles, D. Problems in the assessment of sexual abuse referrals. In: *Sexual Abuse in Children,* W. Holder (Ed.), pp. 58–64. American Humane Association, Englewood, CO (1980).

7. Summit, R. and Kryso, J. Sexual abuse of children: A clinical spectrum. *American Journal of Orthopsychiatry* **48:**237–249 (1978).

8. Sgroi, S. *Handbook of Clinical Intervention in Child Sexual Abuse,* pp. 39–80. Lexington Books, Lexington, MA (1982).

9. Goodwin, J., Sand, D. and Rada, R. Incest hoax: False accusations, false denials. In: *Sexual Abuse in Children,* W. Holder (Ed.), pp. 37–45. American Humane Association, Englewood, CO (1978).

10. Freud, S. *The Sexual Enlightenment of Children.* Collier Books, New York (1971).

11. Rush, F. The Freudian cover-up. In: *The Best Kept Secret: Sexual Abuse of Children.* Prentice Hall, Englewood Cliffs, NJ (1980).

12. Peters, J. Children who are victims of sexual assault and the psychology of offenders. *American Journal of Psychotherapy* **30:**398–421 (1976).

13. Goodwin, J., Sand, D. and Rada, R. In: *Sexual Abuse in Children,* W. Holder (Ed.).

14. Kleinman, J., Interdisciplinary Project on Child Abuse and Neglect, Ann Arbor, MI. Personal communication.

15. Faller, K. Indicators of child sexual abuse. In: *Multidisciplinary Approaches to Child Abuse and Neglect.* University of Michigan Interdisciplinary Project on Child Abuse and Neglect, Ann Arbor, MI (1978).

16. Carlson-Larson, N. Family Sexual Abuse Training Course, University of Minnesota Medical School, Minneapolis, MN (1978).

Suffering in Silence:
The Male Incest Victim

by Maria Nasjleti

Male incest victims have been virtually ignored by most investigators of incest, and little information about them is available in the literature. Large gaps still exist in the social worker's understanding of the dynamics of child sexual abuse.

Since fewer male than female victims of incest come to the attention of law enforcement agencies, most social workers in public agencies have limited knowledge of and experience with male victims [2:1–38]. The study of male incest victims is long overdue. This paper fills part of this gap by examining reasons boys remain silent victims of incest.

The writer's involvement in the Sacramento Child Sexual Abuse Treatment Program has included initiating and coleading a group therapy experience for adolescent male incest victims. The coleader is a male social worker whose professional training and work are similar to the author's.

All of the boys in the group were sexually abused by a relative, and all were court dependents, under the protection and supervision of the juvenile court. The boys were referred to the group by their social workers. Most but not all of them were ordered to be in the group by the juvenile court. They were between the ages of 12 and 17. The group has met once a week for hour-and-a-half sessions, over 22 months. The group dealt with any and all issues related to their sexual abuse, including current struggles to adjust to in-home or out-of-home placement.

Maria Nasjleti is a faculty member of California State University, School of Social Work and is Coordinator of the Sacramento Child Sexual Abuse Treatment Program. "Suffering in Silence: The Male Incest Victim" is reprinted from *Child Welfare,* May 1980, volume LIX, number 5, pp. 269–275. Copyright © 1980, Child Welfare League of America, Inc. Reprinted by permission of the publisher.

The writer found in the boys a consistent pattern of extreme resistance to discussing their molestation experiences. Most of the boys wanted "just to forget it ever happened." Though repeatedly assured that they had done nothing to feel ashamed of, most boys refused to discuss their feelings. When referred for individual therapy, the majority also refused to deal with their sexual abuse experiences. The sex of the therapist had no apparent effect on their attitude.

The author sought to learn more about the psychological factors involved in a boy's difficulty in reporting and discussing his own victimization by consulting with colleagues and child psychiatrists, and by reviewing the literature on the male role in society, male sex offenders, incest and molestation. The research supported the view that in United States culture male children, brought up to be more physically aggressive, self-reliant and independent than female children, probably find it more difficult to report having been molested because boys, unlike girls, are not commonly encouraged to seek help and protection.

VICTIMIZATION AND MASCULINITY

Many books dealing with masculinity in America have been appearing on the market. A common thread is that the culture's definition of masculinity and its expectations for males do not allow expression of feelings of dependency, fear, vulnerability or helplessness in the male. Goldberg discusses the effect the culture's expectations of males have on their physical and psychological health. Among the things males are denied are: being dependent on others, being spontaneous in the expression of feelings, being passive toward aggressiveness other than that from females, or permission to ask for nurturance [3:42–60]. Understandably, these things become difficult for males to do. The result has been that their need to express feelings of fear, vulnerability, helplessness and dependency has gone unmet, and they have suffered silently.

Most boys are encouraged to develop physical strength to protect themselves from others' physical aggression. Consider the games and toys designed specifically for boys. Most are intended to develop aggressiveness, self-assertiveness, competitiveness and self-reliance. The underlying message is that to be nonaggressive, nonassertive, noncompetitive and nonself-reliant is not masculine. From early childhood boys learn that masculinity means not depending on anyone, not being weak, not being passive, not being a loser in confrontation, in short, not being a victim.

EFFECTS OF SEDUCTION BY A SIGNIFICANT ADULT FEMALE

Professionals and the public in general react either with disbelief or passive acceptance to the sexual abuse of boys by adult females. There exists a myth that seduction of the male child is a positive sexual experience for the boy. The sexual relationship between the adolescent boy and the wife of his basketball coach depicted in the movie "The Last Picture Show" speaks to this American sexual fantasy. However, clinical observations of the effects of seduction of a male child by his mother, mother surrogate, or other significant adult female indicate the following findings:

1) Rapists are often found to have had sexual or sexualized relationships with their mothers [4:1-16].
2) Boys who have had sexual relationships with their mothers and develop mental disorders often become schizophrenic [6:100].
3) Incestuous fathers are often found to have had stimulating relationships with their mothers [1:203-216].
4) Some homosexuals are said to have chosen homosexuality as a defense against their sexual feelings for a seductive mother [5:218-226].
5) Sexuality for child molesters is not usually the primary factor involved in their molesting behavior. It is instead the arena in which psychosocial issues such as their own childhood seduction are played out [4:16].

In short, seduction of a boy by his mother, mother surrogate or significant adult female in his life is detrimental to a boy's psychosocial development. The negative effects of such sexual experience are numerous, and most endanger the well-being of women and children, who become victims of men who, as boys, were sexually abused by women.

MALES' DENIAL OF HELPLESSNESS

Reacting passively to physical aggression of any kind except from females is perceived by males as a feminine trait. Their resistance to asking for help stems from a reluctance to identify themselves as helpless or passive.

Boys also equate passivity with homosexuality. Homosexual activity is considered by most heterosexual American males to be abhorrent or shameful. The connection between homosexuality and passivity in the American male's mind is unfortunate; reporting that they have been victims of homosexual assaults is to boys tantamount to admitting that they are homosexual, even though they were forced into such activity. Fearing that their masculinity will be questioned or challenged if they report such molestation, most choose to remain silent.

The author believes that boys' reluctance, resistance or refusal to report their sexual victimization may be related to shame at not having been the dominant person controlling the molestation situations. From an early age, males are taught that they must strive for dominance because it is "manly." Understandably, a boy does not easily admit having been in situations in which he had no control over what was happening to him, and in which he was not the dominant person.

Male professionals too often disbelieve a boy's report of sexual abuse. A police officer once told the writer that he found it difficult to believe a boy "could be raped" because "a boy could prevent being raped if he really wanted to." Placing the responsibility for the rape on the rape victim has long been a way for some to escape their own feelings of vulnerability and powerlessness. To accept as true the reported sexual assaults forces these persons to deal with their own vulnerability to victimization, or their potential to victimize someone else.

SELF-CONCEPT AS VICTIMS OF INCEST

Evidently many psychosocial and emotional factors play a part in a boy's unwillingness to reveal sexual victimization. Boys who are being sexually abused feel, at the least, ambivalence and, at the worst, dread about reporting the abuse. Reporting his own victimization may activate in him one or more of the following fears:

1) Since he was unable to protect himself, he fears being considered a "sissy" or "unmanly." Fearing that he may be ridiculed and rejected if he identifies himself as a victim, he may choose not to report the abuse.

2) If he has been homosexually molested, he may fear that people will think he is homosexual, and he is likely to fear becoming homosexual. Such fears arise out of boys' belief that homosexual molestation can cause homosexuality.

3) If he is being sexually abused by a woman, he may hesitate to report it if he thinks his complaint will bring his masculinity into question. Boys often assume such a complaint will be interpreted as evidence of sexual abnormality.

4) Boys often fear that having sex with the mother is indicative of their having a mental illness. Because mothers are viewed as nonsexual beings in this culture, incapable of sexually abusing their children, boys molested by their mothers often assume responsibility for their own molestation.

5) Boys fear that no one will believe their report of sexual abuse because they think molestation of boys is so uncommon that most people simply find such a report difficult to accept. This idea is fostered by lack of coverage of the topic in the news media.

6) Boys fear reporting being sexually abused because asking for help makes them ashamed that they were unable to protect themselves.

7) Boys fear that nothing will be done to stop their sexual abuse by a woman because they believe that most people think such sexual activity is not harmful to the boy.

8) Boys fear that reporting their own sexual victimization may mean risking their safety and well-being. This fear is based in reality, as many times relatives threaten the boys they are molesting with physical harm if they report the abuse. Fear of injury is one of the major reasons boys wait until they are in adolescence to report having been sexually abused. Their size and weight then allow them to feel less physically vulnerable.

BOYS' FEELINGS REGARDING DISCLOSURE

To test these conjectures the writer administered a short questionnaire to the nine boys who were in the group 3 months after its inception. By this time the boys were more comfortable talking about their molestation experiences with each other and with the group leaders. The questionnaire sought first to identify the boys' feelings regarding disclosure of their sexual victimization, and second, to identify their perceptions of public opinion about the sexual abuse of boys. The questionnaire consisted of 10 questions relating to the circumstances of the sexual abuse and/or their feelings about disclosing it.

The majority of the boys said they felt ashamed and scared to report or disclose their sexual abuse to other persons. Once they made the decision to disclose their abuse, most were angered by the disbelief they encountered. Several said their greatest fears were justified by persons' reactions. They think most persons don't believe boys are molested, since the public seldom hears about such cases, and many think boys could prevent such abuse.

Although this small sample cannot claim statistical significance, the findings do demonstrate an overall concurrence among the boys, and their responses support the views advanced in this article.

THE NEED FOR CHANGE

What does it indicate about our society that male children tell us they cannot look for protection because they have been taught that they are responsible for protecting themselves? The writer submits that there is a real need to reexamine society's role expectations of male children. Unrealistic demands and emotional restrictions on boys create a climate conducive to their victimization, and in turn their victimization of others.

Professionals have several responsibilities in regard to this problem: first, a responsibility to explore ways to facilitate a boy's disclosure of sexual abuse; second, a responsibility to spread information found useful, so that a greater number of children can be helped; third, a responsibility to make the general public more aware of the disastrous consequences of current socialization patterns for male children. Parents should be taught that boys need as much affection and nurturing as girls, and equal permission to express feelings of dependency, fear, vulnerability and helplessness. Acknowledging that male and female children have those emotional needs in common is the first step toward rearing them more equally, psychologically speaking. Only then can professionals say that they have attempted to break the intergenerational cycle of sexual abuse.

REFERENCES

1. Cormier, B.; Kennedy, M., and Sangowitz, J. "Psychodynamics of Father-Daughter Incest," Canadian Psychiatry, VII (1962).

2. DeFrancis, Vincent, "Protecting the Child Victim of Sex Crimes Committed by Adults," Denver: American Humane Association, Children's Division, 1969.

3. Goldberg, Herb. The Hazards of Being Male: Surviving the Myth of Masculine Privilege. New York: New American Library, 1977.

4. Groth, Nicholas A., and Burgess, Ann W. "Child Sexual Assault: Dominance, Authority and Aggression," paper presented at the American Association for Psychiatric Services to Children, San Francisco, 1976.

5. Langsley, Donald; Schwartz, Michael, and Fairbairn, Robert. "Father-Son Incest," Comprehensive Psychiatry, IX, 3 (May 1968).

6. Wahl, Charles W. "The Psychodynamic of Consummated Maternal Incest," Archives of General Psychiatry, III (August 1960).

Defense Mechanisms Used by Sexually Abused Children

by Christine Adams-Tucker

Studies of groups of sexually molested children have described the immediate and long-term effects of their abuse—symptoms, diagnosis and problem areas projected into their future adult lives. Findings from groups convey valuable descriptive data on molested children, particularly on how much and for how long they suffer psychological harm from sexual abuse during childhood. Individual case reports of sexually victimized children deepen our perspective by constructing an unfolding scenario of the coping strategies employed by each child. In such reports, inferences are made about psychic defenses that aid or obstruct children in grappling with their abuse. Defenses are ordinarily studied as part of a larger motivational or psychodynamic exploration, but taken by themselves, defenses make a good beginning toward the dynamic assessment of a child.

This article discusses the psychic defense strategies used by a group of 27 children, ranging in age from 2½ to 15½, who were sexually molested. By looking at them both individually and as a group, we may be helped to understand not only what sexually abused children suffer but also how they internally defend against their unhappiness.

METHODS

The 27 children—five boys and 22 girls—were given psychiatric evaluations at a child guidance clinic in 1978. In most cases the sexual abuse, known prior to the evaluation, constituted a basis for the child's

Christine Adams-Tucker is a physician in private practice in child, adolescent and adult psychiatry in Louisville, Kentucky and a member of the clinical faculty, University of Louisville. "Defense Mechanisms Used by Sexually Abused Children" is reprinted from *Children Today* January/February 1985, volume 14, number 1, pp. 9–12, 34. Reprinted by permission of the author.

referral. In a few instances, however, the sexual abuse became evident only during the evaluation. Each evaluation was performed over a consecutive 3-hour period on one day. Parents (or other primary care-takers) were seen, both together with their children and individually, in all cases where it was possible for parents to get to the clinic. All of the children were seen individually. Evaluations were performed by social workers, psychologists, general psychiatry residents or child psychiatry fellows. Other professionals on the staff of the child guidance clinic collaborated in formulating diagnostic impressions and recommending dispositions.

Two procedures were used. The children's charts were examined retrospectively to glean information about their defenses and use of defense mechanisms in relation to sexual victimization. In most instances, explicit references to defenses could be culled from written evaluations and psychological test reports. The types of defense mechanisms that I coded included all of those listed in the *Comprehensive Textbook of Psychiatry*—narcissistic, immature, neurotic and mature.[1] The other procedure involved interviews with clinicians to corroborate and amplify what had been written about clinical evaluations and psychological testing.

After enumerating the subtypes of defense mechanisms (narcissistic, immature, neurotic and mature), the types of defense mechanisms were analyzed according to gender, age, severity of psychopathology and duration of abuse for each child. Moreover, for each child, coping strategies were examined while comparing the time elapsed between molestation and psychiatric evaluation, the identity of his or her molester and the level of support from caring adults.

In labelling the defense mechanisms, the children's behaviors, thoughts and emotions during evaluations were viewed in conjunction with accepted theories about defense mechanisms. For example, the defense mechanism of sexualization (a neurotic type) was inferred from the behavior of an 8-year-old girl who, during her psychiatric evaluation, continually flipped her dress up, showing the male evaluator her panties and asking if he liked them. When asked about her sexual abuse, she said emphatically that she was "hot" and asked to remove all of her clothes and sit on the evaluator's lap. Similarly, the mechanism of projection (an immature type) was discerned from the recurrent thought of a 4-year-old girl that her mother would get mad and blame her for the sexual molestation by her father, and the mechanisms of regression and schizoid fantasy (immature types) were inferred from the emotions of a 14-year-old girl, raped by her step-father, who alternated between muteness and sobbing with rageful, hostile screams.

FINDINGS

Psychiatric diagnoses, spanning a continuum from adjustment reactions to psychosis, were recorded for 26 children; one child, a boy, had no mental disorder.

Sixteen of the 22 girls were molested by fathers or father surrogates, and four of the five boys were molested by boy age-mates. Most types of sexual abuse involved an adult's genital or manual contact with the genitalia of the child (54 percent). Almost one-third of the types were oral-genital abuse (31 percent), with the molester forcing the child to perform fellatio.

Preschool children had problems with sleeping, nightmares and bodily complaints; school-aged children with masturbation, school and home behavior problems and withdrawal. Adolescents were more often depressed and suicidal than younger children. The duration of abuse for these youngsters was highly varied, ranging from one-time victimization to eight years of recurrent sexual molestation, with a mean of 2.7 years.

The changes in the children's self-concept following molestation were overwhelmingly negative. They lost self-esteem and felt guilt and shame. Only one child, a 7-year-old girl, showed an upsurge in self-esteem. She regarded the molestation by her father as a sign that she had been singled out as special among her siblings. A 3½-year-old girl, who voiced much anger with her father for his abuse, showed no loss or gain in self-esteem.

The children evidenced core value conflicts, reflecting their struggle to come to grips with the abuse and the degree to which they felt responsible for their victimization. Their conflicts differed depending upon whether the molester was a part of the immediate family or an outsider. Father-molested children most often experienced conflicts over family loyalty versus personal autonomy, blaming oneself versus blaming the father, and blaming the father versus blaming the other parent. Children victimized by peers, neighbors and distant relatives also evidenced conflicts over blaming oneself versus blaming the molester as well as over parents' blaming the child for the abuse versus parents' blaming the molester.

DEFENSES

One child, a 3½-year-old boy, was said to have used no defense mechanisms and three other children (two girls and one boy, ages 3½, 7 and 7½), showed predominantly "undefended anxiety" with Gross Stress Reactions—restlessness, increased motor activity, constant sighing, tremulousness and increased frequency of urination. Narcissistic defense mechanisms were evident for 13 children; immature mechanisms for 25; neurotic for 15; and mature for 5 (see Table 1).

Table 1.

Defense Mechanisms	Girls (N=22) N (%)	Boys (N=5) N (%)
Gross Stress Reaction	2 (9)	1 (20)
No Defense Mechanisms	0	1 (20)
Narcissistic	11 (50)	2 (40)
Denial	11 (50)	2 (40)
Distortion	2 (9)	1 (20)
Delusional Projection	0	1 (20)
Immature	21 (95)	4 (80)
Introjection	17 (77)	3 (60)
Acting Out	10 (45)	3 (60)
Schizoid Fantasy	4 (18)	0
Somatization	4 (18)	0
Projection	3 (13)	1 (20)
Passive-Aggressive	2 (9)	0
Regression	2 (9)	0
Blocking	0	1 (20)
Hyponchondriasis	1 (4)	0
Neurotic	14 (63)	1 (20)
Sexualization	7 (32)	1 (20)
Displacement	5 (23)	1 (20)
Controlling	4 (18)	1 (20)
Reaction Formation	4 (18)	0
Somatization	4 (18)	0
Dissociation	0	1 (20)
Externalization	0	1 (20)
Mature	4 (18)	1 (20)
Suppression	3 (14)	1 (20)
Altruism	1 (4)	0

Gender. Boys employed predominantly immature defense mechanisms and only one boy (a 4-year-old) used any neurotic coping maneuvers. Girls, too, employed many immature mechanisms but they also adopted a variety of neurotic ones. Boys used acting-out as a coping maneuver somewhat more than girls did, but these boys had been molested most often by peers. On the other hand, girls exclusively employed the mechanisms of schizoid fantasy, passive-aggression, somatization and reaction formation.

Age. The youngest children, the preschoolers, had the fewest identified defenses of all age groups. School-aged children coped with their sexual abuse through the most wide-ranging variety of mental mechanisms. Denial was found prevalently in this age group, and a majority used introjection. The foremost neurotic type of defense mechanism employed was sexualization, found in both re-enactment behavior and in post-traumatic play.

Adolescents, from age 12 to 15½, were more restricted than school-aged children in the variety of defense mechanisms they evidenced. Immature coping maneuvers were most frequent, especially acting-out and introjection.

Severity of Psychopathology. Severely disturbed preschoolers and school-aged children used relatively many and more varied defense maneuvers compared to children who were less emotionally impaired. The seven adolescents who were seriously disturbed employed fewer and more restricted defenses than their younger school-age counterparts. Regression, schizoid fantasy, acting-out and introjection were used primarily by these most distressed adolescents.

Duration of Abuse. No pattern (independent of the child's age) emerged in the defense mechanisms employed when a brief duration of sexual abuse (less than six months) was compared to a more lengthy duration of victimization (four to eight years). Acting-out, however, was seen more often in children who were victimized over a longer period. Thus, very young children coped with their abuse by using similar defensive functions whether they had been abused only once or over a 4-year period. Teenagers, too, used the same defensive maneuvers regardless of the duration of the abuse.

Time Elapsed before Evaluation. Children who were abused by their fathers or father surrogates did not receive psychiatric help until an average of nearly three years after the molestation occurred. When the perpetrators were peers, neighbors and more distant relatives, children obtained evaluations earlier—an average of four months following the molestation. Children victimized by perpetrators other than their fathers used acting-out, denial, introjection and schizoid fantasy as their main defenses. Boys molested by their peers showed the most undefended anxiety of any group. When they did use defensive coping techniques, these often were directed outward or anxiety was withheld from consciousness via such mechanisms as acting-out, projection and dissociation.

Depending on their value conflicts surrounding the abuse, father-molested children used varied defenses. Those who valued family loyalty and who abused and denigrated themselves used denial and introjection a great deal. On the other hand, those who showed more autonomy (less self-abasement) and who blamed their fathers for the abuse more than they blamed themselves had little denial and used acting-out far more frequently than their counterparts. Interestingly, the mean time elapsed before help was sought was greatest among the children who blamed themselves for their father's molestation (3.6 years) compared to those who blamed their fathers for the abuse (1.5 years). Sexualization was used as frequently by each group.

Support from Caring Adults. The support each child received from a close adult following disclosure of the molestation affected the degree of conflict faced by each child which, in turn, affected the defense mechanisms employed. Children who went unsupported for lengthy periods were most often victims of father-daughter incest who evidenced a high degree of family loyalty and who blamed themselves for the molestation. By and large, they denied the incest had created any problems for them and introjected the belief of their abusive fathers that the incest episodes were all right.

Children who received immediate support and aid from a parent were found in both the father-molested group and the group molested by others. Those abused by fathers showed much personal autonomy and blamed their molesters, even though they introjected some degree of culpability. Children molested by others showed Gross Stress Reactions and fewer defense mechanisms. Even children who had received support only recently (following a lengthy period of no support) fared better psychically; they were more likely to be autonomous and to blame their molester. However, some children who had received support only recently had developed severe psychopathology and rigid and immature defenses of acting-out and schizoid fantasy through the long period of non-support.

DISCUSSION

The children in the study varied their coping techniques for dealing with sexual abuse in ways that depended more on their age at the time of their psychiatric evaluation than on factors of gender or duration of sexual abuse.

Defense against anxiety was both minimal and primative in comparatively less disturbed preschoolers. The very young displayed either unbound anxiety (Gross Stress Reactions) or primitive, less sophisticated (in a developmental sense) mechanisms that dichotomize psychic energy into "your fault/my fault"; anxiety directed to others or to self. They defended themselves in ways consistent with immaturity of emotion, cognition and behavior. More disturbed preschoolers were "pseudomature" in their coping, adopting defensive maneuvers more similar in variety and sophistication to those of their school-aged counterparts. Perhaps the stress of sexual abuse compelled intrapsychic strategies to "jump the gun" when very young children, being overwhelmed, attempted to cope by using ways beyond their years, forcing ego development to leap ahead in time. However, their defensive precocity did not enable them to master nor to adapt to the stressful event of rape at a young age.

Each school-aged child, using a variety of coping devices, attempted to find a few mechanisms or combination of mechanisms to dispel or reduce anxiety. Such wide-ranging diversity observed in the business of coping may reflect the augmented capabilities of the more developed ego but still did not enable this age group of children to succeed in mastering the cumulative stresses of sexual victimization. Of importance to clinicians serving these youngsters is the finding that more latency-aged children resorted to sexualization as a means of coping than did older or younger children. As a result, I believe that their sexual latency came to abrupt termination, if, indeed, it ever had a prior existence. The psychic insult with which they must deal is sexual in nature, after all, and their response is one of sexualization.

While small children tried out coping mechanisms that were beyond their age level, teenagers regressed and dealt with sexual victimization through a restricted number of rather primitive defenses—the narcissistic and immature. Their regression was compulsive and debilitating and might better be called "ego distortions," which resemble normal coping during periods of stress but which solidify as a way of life in which ego development is chronically immature but relatively unchangeable.[2] That conclusion is suggested by the severe psychopathology seen in the adolescent age group.

Interactions can be identified in the children's coping strategies according to the time elapsed between molestation and psychiatric evaluation, the identity of the molester and the level of support from caring adults.

The father-molested children coped with the abuse differently depending upon two external and related factors: the level of support received which, in turn, influenced the time lapse before evaluation. Non-support made itself known in the adult's failure to obtain early and prompt psychiatric care for the child. Children who went unsupported for a long period valued their autonomy little and placed a major value upon keeping the secret of incest and preserving a semblance of family unity. Since no communications had come forth that blamed the father, they felt they were at fault. They may rightfully blame the mother for some aspects of their victimization because they told her and she did nothing, or they may wrongfully blame their mother for not knowing, for her lack of omniscience in knowing all that happens to her child—"She should have known even though I never told her." In this manner they displaced their anger with their molester onto their mother.

These youngsters regarded their fathers as infallible, denied their lack of trust in them and denied that the abuse may have been deleterious to them. They introjected the belief that "what Dad did was OK" and acted-out most often against themselves with suicide attempts. To some degree, the properly functioning ego necessitates that children rely on a notion of infallibility and trustworthiness of a parent. Their egos are not mature enough to blame the one whom they had learned to trust, especially where there is no disruption of the incestuous *status quo*. These children were distrustful of the "bad" molester but remained trusting of the "infallible father." They fragmented their view of their father-molesters. Such a fragmenting operation of the mind has been described as a vertical splitting in which mental images of a good and a bad parent are compartmentalized—isolated from one another—and yet are simultaneously coexistent.[3]

Parents who supported their father-molested children sought help for them earlier. These children's conflicts revealed their value of their own autonomy over loyalty to the family unit, and they vituperatively blamed their fathers for their victimization. They were not without problems, however, and martialled a host of defenses to grapple with the conflicts surrounding their core values. On the whole, they did not deny the problems brought on by the incest, nor did they deny the anger and the betrayal of trust they felt by their fathers' actions. They acted out their conflicts far more than those who were not supported. These acting-out behaviors were directed toward the self—as with suicide attempts—but also included aggressive behavior toward others, such as running away, abusing pets and destroying property. It appeared that, with less denial, the "vertical splits" in their view of their fathers were more in conflict even though the children appeared to have stronger egos than those in the self-abasing group. These children internalized and identified with the breach of impulse control manifested by their father-molesters and they, too, acted out. Such impulsivity as a way of life leads them to character disorders and maladaptive behaviors.

The youngsters sexually abused by peers, neighbors and distant relatives, who were most likely to be supported by both parents who quickly sought help for them, were more successful at directing anxiety away from the self. Because of their distance from the molester, these children were usually able to blame the perpetrator or, at least, to act out with other than self-punitive behaviors or dam up the anxiety by blocking or denying that much had happened to cause them distress. However, they did not escape self-blame entirely, and this can be compounded if parents blame the victim for the circumstances of the abuse.

In all of the foregoing, I did not intend to suggest that any onus is on children who respond pathologically to being sexually abused. In fact, their being sexually abused is viewed as a needless victimization and a deleterious experience from which children require protection and for which they need therapeutic aid.

Sexual victimization is a psychic injury that requires coping throughout the life of a child. His or, more commonly, her ego is constantly rechallenged with trauma as development ensues, even if actual seduction has ended. The events and memories of them must be grappled with in a different way throughout each stage of childhood.

Coming to terms with sexual violation of the self, be it by relatives, strangers, adults or other children, is a difficult task for a child. The core value conflicts, and the defense mechanisms martialled in coping with them, reveal that many victimized children muster many assets and display ego strengths. They blow the whistle. Many receive quick support from their parent(s). And they often obtain psychiatric help that dispels fear and provides relief from their stresses. However, as seen in these 27 children, ego strengths alone are not sufficient to dispel psychic debilitation. Lengthy clinical remediation is necessary so that these youngsters will not pass on to their children sexual cruelty and victimization.

REFERENCES

1. H. I. Kaplan, A. M. Freedman and B. J. Sadock, *Comprehensive Textbook of Psychiatry, III.* Baltimore. Williams-Wilkins Co., 1980.

2. M. Gitelson, "On Ego Distortion," *International Journal of Psychoanalysis, 39,* 1958 and M. Brenman, "On Teasing and Being Teased and the Problem of Moral Masochism," *The Psychoanalytic Study of the Child, 7,* 1952.

3. I. I. Shengold, "Child Abuse and Deprivation: Soul Murder," *Journal of the American Psychoanal. Assoc., 27*(3), 1979.

SECTION IV

Professional Perspectives

Introduction

Following an incidence of sexual abuse, child victims often come in contact with an array of professionals: physicians, attorneys, teachers, social workers, law enforcement officers, psychologists. Ideally, all of them have the welfare of the child as their primary goal. Each operates from a different educational bias and societal role, and this section examines some of these different professional perspectives. It begins with Richard Riggs's "Incest: The School's Role," in which the author identifies the school's responsibilities for intervention, treatment, and prevention of child sexual abuse. Still focusing on the educational aspect, "You Can Help a Sexually Abused Child," by Janet Rosenzweig, specifically addresses the classroom teacher by offering direct advice on how to identify and handle cases of suspected abuse.

The next article, "Sexually Abused Children: Identification and Suggestions for Intervention," by Marla Brassard, Ann Tyler, and Thomas Kehle, can aid the school psychologist in developing skills to identify and interview victims of abuse and to become familiar with referral policies. The unique position of the school psychologist as the liason between home, school, and social agency is stressed.

In "The Play Technique: Diagnosing the Sexually Abused Child," Ann French Clark and Jane Bingham further expound the diagnostic aspect of sexual abuse. The paper details age-appropriate behavioral and verbal responses that might be evidence of abuse, suggests different aids to use when establishing communication with a sexually abused child, and shows examples of how children, through drawings, can express their emotional difficulties.

Lucy Berliner and Mary Kay Barbieri's article, "The Testimony of the Child Victim of Sexual Assault," concerns itself with the impediments to establishing the credibility of the child as a witness in his/her own behalf. This article offers solutions to overcoming these obstacles and provides methods for safeguarding against the psychological hazards that may result when a child appears in court.

The final article, "When Systems Fail: Protecting the Victim of Child Sexual Abuse" by Dr. Vincent J. Fontana, provides a critique of the entire "system" of people involved in offering service to a sexually abused child. The author discusses a number of factors that create an overall damaging effect on the very children they were designed to help. He makes an appeal for a more coordinated effort, on the part of all the agencies concerned, to prevent further harm to these children.

Incest: The School's Role

by Richard S. Riggs

Incest has been a significant health problem throughout history and today adversely affects an estimated 10 to 20 million persons in this country alone.[1] The responsibility for intervention, treatment, and ultimate prevention of incest lies with those in the helping professions including the school system and its personnel.

Medical literature is replete with studies pertaining to the harmful effects of incestuous relationships and has encouraged health professionals to face the reality of incest being a serious health problem. Many popular magazines such as *Family Circle, Woman's Day, Ladies Home Journal, Redbook,* plus other periodicals have contained articles written by women who themselves were victims of incest. A review of health education journals, however, reveals an apparent lack of attention given to the incest/sexual abuse problem, a significant health issue in present day society.

DEFINITIONS

The definitions for incest as used in the literature extend over a continuum of sexually related behaviors between children and adults. A review of the literature reveals that incest may be defined only in terms of sexual intercourse. For example, Lustig et al define incest as "overt sexual intercourse occurring between members of a group who are not permitted by their society to marry."[2] Justice and Justice define incest as "any sexual activity—intimate physical contact that is sexually arousing—between nonmarried members of a family."[3] For-

---

Richard S. Riggs is Associate Professor of Health Education at the University of Kentucky. "Incest: The School's Role" is reprinted from *Journal of School Health,* August 1982, volume 52, number 6, pp. 365–370. Copyright © 1982. American School Health Association, Kent, OH, 44240. Reprinted by permission of the publisher.

ward defines incest as "any overtly sexual contact between people who are either closely related or perceive themselves closely related."[1]

The manner in which incest as a form of sexual behavior is categorized is another issue. The term may refer to a separate form of behavior, as a component of sexual abuse, sexual misuse exploitation.[4] For the purposes of the paper, the authors use the definition as stated by the National Center on Child Abuse and Neglect. They refer to incest as an "intrafamily sexual abuse" and define it as:

> that abuse which is perpetrated on a child by a member of that child's family group and includes not only sexual intercourse, but also any act designed to stimulate a child sexually, or to use a child for sexual stimulation, either of the perpetrator or of another person.[5]

THE SCHOOL'S INVOLVEMENT

The schools of this country have a significant influence on the lives and development of children and must be attuned to factors which adversely affect or interfere with the child's learning and development. The school's role goes beyond that of education; the school can also serve as a resource in the community for meeting the various needs of children and youth.

Schools are being encouraged, in part by legal mandates, to become more involved in the entire spectrum of child abuse and neglect including the problem of incest. Since incestuous relationships ultimately adversely affect the community, they are community problems and must be dealt with and solved by community efforts. Often the school can help with the incest problem in ways no other institution or agency can.

Giarretto states the average age of incest victims is 10 years old.[6] With the familiarity teachers have with their pupils, often the teacher or nurse knows or suspects something is amiss with a child long before overt symptoms become apparent to others. Through teacher and nurse observations, recording health histories, screening tests, measuring growth and development, diagnostic tests, conferences with other school personnel, conferences with the child and his/her parents, school personnel are in strategic positions to detect, intervene and ultimately prevent further occurrence of incest.

School personnel have both a moral and a legal obligation to help students experiencing problems and/or manifesting behavior indicative of being traumatized. Schools must initiate action to prevent the occurrence of incest, which is harmful to the healthful development of children. Additionally, there is a legal mandate which specifically requires the reporting of suspected child abuse (which typically includes incestuous behavior) with the proper authorities. More specifically, most if not all states have reporting laws which single out school personnel to report abuse/incest. For those who report in good faith, immunity clauses provide protection against legal liability for reporting. Those who fail to report abuse/incest incur liability for their negligence. Generally, because parents regard school personnel as non-threatening and supportive, teachers are permitted to deal with crisis situations such as abuse/incest through referrals of family members to community agencies.

Incest has been referred to as a "crime our society abhors in the abstract, but tolerates in reality . . . in part because it is the final component of the maltreatment syndrome that we have yet to face headon."[7] The areas in which the school and its personnel have responsibilities are: awareness of the incest problem; observation and detection; reporting and referrals; counseling and followup; and prevention.

AWARENESS OF THE INCEST PROBLEM

Incest persists in part because many persons, including health professionals, are unwilling to consider the reality of incest. The fact is that incest is a form of sexual behavior practiced by a significant number of persons in this country and throughout the world. Justice and Justice suggests incest is largely ignored due to:

1. The taboo against talking about it.
2. The refusal by physicians, clergy, relatives, and neighbors who may be aware that incest is going on in a family to report it or become involved.
3. The laws in almost half the states that fail to specify sexual abuse as one of the forms of abuse of children that must be reported.
4. The fiction that only the poor and the pathological engage in incest.
5. The attitude that nothing can be done to prevent it from occurring or to rehabilitate families if it does occurr.[3]

Other reasons for failing to deal openly with incest are related to attitudes and myths. Some believe incest is just too dirty to think about, that it is disgusting and incompatible with socially acceptable behavior. Incest to others is only a fantasy in the mind of some demented person and therefore not a reality. Others believe incest occurs only in isolated "back woods" communities. Or the perpetrator is a kinky sex fiend because "normal" people would not engage in sexual relationships with their children. Or the child either overtly or covertly seduces the parent/adult and it is therefore the child who is at fault, not the adult.

The reality is that all of these statements are myths which can be dispelled by factual information. The fact is that incest does occur in most, if not all, communities representing all segments of socioeconomic groups. The perpetrator of incest is usually "normal" and not a kinky sexual being. Incest does occur in extremely isolated situations in which the child may have seduced the adult; however, in the overwhelming majority of instances, the adult seduced the child. Most experts would agree that the adult in the incestuous relationship:

> always infringes on the rights of the child, overthrows the child's right to be protected from harmful interference with its psychological, social, and sometimes physical development.[8]

A number of factors, including the women's movement in particular, has led to increased numbers of women revealing that they were victims of incest. Other data sources reveal that, as more states pass effective legislation for reporting sexual abuse/incest, the extent of the incest problem is becoming better known. The increased incidence of reported incestuous relationships are believed to be actual increases in the number of instances and not merely a higher instance of reporting.[3] As is true for all forms of abuse and maltreatment of children, the actual number of cases is unknown and therefore only speculative estimates.

Zaphiris states that an overwhelming number of incestuous families occupy the workload of protective service practitioners, and this could be one of the indicators that the incidence of incestuous relationships may be more widespread than previously thought.[9] Others specify the number of incest cases to be of staggering dimensions. Woodbury and Schwartz state that the number of incest cases was "one in a million in 1940, one in 100 people in 1950, and one in 20 in 1970."[10] The American Humane Association estimates that 100,000 children are sexually abused each year.[11] Today, Zaphiris believes the incidence of incest to be 2 to 3 people per 100 population.[12] Regardless of the speculative estimates, researchers are finding sexual abuse/incest to be one of the most underreported and undiagnosed type of child abuse.[13] One study in Los Angeles revealed approximately 90% of incest cases were not reported.[14] Therefore, estimates of the problem or numbers of reported cases are in reality only the "tip of the iceberg."

OBSERVATION AND DETECTION

The classroom teacher and the school nurse are in strategic positions to detect incest involving a school-age child. The classroom teacher observes his/her students each school day over the course of the school year. They become quite knowledgeable about their students and most often will know when a particular child has a problem or is manifesting anxiety over a problem. Broadhurst,[15] Baker,[16] Tormes,[17] and others[18-20] have compiled lists of indicators typically manifested by victims of sexual abuse/incest. Selected pertinent indicators for school personnel to consider are:

PHYSICAL INDICATORS OF INCEST

1. A sexually transmitted disease in young children.
2. Complaints of pain and/or itching in the genital areas.
3. Evidence of trauma in the genital areas.
4. Unusual odors around the genital areas.
5. Torn, stained, or bloody underclothing.
6. Difficulty in walking or sitting.
7. Pregnancy in young child.

BEHAVIORAL INDICATORS OF INCEST

1. A child behaving in an unusually seductive manner with peers or adults.
2. An unwillingness to undress or participate in physical education classes.
3. Reluctance on the part of the child to go home after school.
4. Frequent absences from school justified by the male caretaker/parent.
5. Withdrawn, infantile behavior, or the child engages in fantasies.
6. Overly sophisticated knowledge and interest in sexual acts and vocabulary.
7. Expression by the child that he/she has been sexually involved with an adult.
8. Expressions by other children that the child told them of the sexual experience.
9. Manifestations through the child's school work, art, poems, and stories of unusual sexual behaviors or themes.
10. Repeated attempts of the child to run away from home.
11. The child turns to the use of drugs/alcohol.
12. Poor peer relationships.

FAMILIAL AND/OR PARENTAL INDICATORS OF INCEST

1. Jealous or overly protective of child.
2. Isolation/alienation of child and family members within the community.

3. Frequent absences from home by one of the caretakers/parents of the child.

4. A pattern of rigid, restrictive control by the father of one or more of the female children.

5. A father whose behavior is characterized by frequent drinking or by alcoholism and a history of abusive, unfeeling treatment of other family members.

6. An inordinate participation by the father in the dynamics of family life and a concomitant over-dependency on him by the mother.

Overt incest symptoms manifested by the child are generally obvious and can be detected by most persons who are willing to focus on those indicators. Covert symptoms require a knowledge and understanding of the child and his/her usual behavior. Because the child is in close personal contact with the teacher and school nurse, both overt and covert symptoms can more easily be connected to a specific problem.

In many instances, the school nurse can detect incest easier than other school personnel. Frequently, the classroom teacher will refer a child to the nurse for an explanation of a particular behavior, for a second opinion or to confirm a suspicion. Also, the school nurse is often approached by students who would not ordinarily go to their teachers or another adult. These students view the nurse as a caring, supportive, nonjudgemental person concerned for their welfare. These students may be victims of incest themselves or have confided in peers who in turn come to the school nurse and tell her of the incestuous relationship. The fact is that the school nurse is perceived as being the person one goes to when they are "hurting" and the nurse will help the hurt to go away.

For many of the same reasons, the parents—and specifically the mother of the abused child—may be more inclined to confide in the school nurse and share information with her they would unlikely share with anyone else. This may occur during a home visit or during a parent-teacher/nurse conference in the school. The mother may be blunt and reveal that she knows or strongly suspects incest; or she may make vague, nonspecific references to the fact that the daughter is involved in an incestuous relationship. Often, the mother will be relieved that the nurse knows since she herself has felt helpless to intervene. Regardless of the source of information, the teacher or nurse will need to discuss with the child and/or parents the situation and the school's involvement. Broadhurst[15] and Keller[21] have identified guidelines to follow while school personnel interview the child and parents:

1. Reassure the child and parents the interview is confidential and is being held in private.

2. Inform the child and parents of the school's legal responsibility to report.
3. Be open, honest, professional, and use language appropriate for understanding by the child and parents.
4. Do not try to place blame nor make judgements as to who is at fault.
5. Do not try to prove incest's occurrence by removing the child's clothing.
6. Do not probe for answers the child or parent are unwilling to provide. Allow the interviewee to talk as much about the relationship as they want.
7. Be supportive and let parent and child know that the school is a support system for the family.
8. Anticipate reactions to incest's becoming known to others. The child and parents may become quite angry or highly emotional. The interviewer should not display shock or other visible reactions to the situation.
9. Inform the parents and/or child of any future action the school will/must take in the situation.

REPORTING AND REFERRALS

When school personnel suspect a child is involved in an incestuous relationship, they have a moral and legal obligation to file a report with the proper authorities. The law is clear that one need not wait until there is absolute proof of such a relationship, but only needs to suspect incest is occurring. If the teacher or nurse delays reporting, the child is left potentially at risk for further sexual abuse. The actual process of filing a report may be difficult for some individuals because incest is a sensitive issue, and filing a report usually involves the teacher/nurse more deeply in the case. The educator should keep in mind his/her concern for the welfare of the child and remember that filing a report is not an accusation against the parent or child, but merely the report of a suspicion. The child protection agency is then legally responsible to investigate the situation and take the necessary steps to ensure the welfare of the child and family.

The report should be made as soon as there is reason to believe a child is involved in incest. Some states' statutes specify the time interval between the teacher's suspicion and the time of filing a report. Delaying a report only serves to prevent more immediate helpful intervention in the family crisis. The report should be made to child welfare or other local child protection agency as specified in local school policies or legal statutes. If such agencies are unavailable, one should notify the local health department, police department or call a child abuse or crisis hotline. Since the reporting procedures vary according to locale, each school system must have written policies and procedures specifying specific action to take in cases of suspected incest/sexual abuse.

Teacher/nurse documentation of suspected incest should begin as soon as suspicion is aroused. Care should be taken to record the dates and specific events/observations pertinent to that which aroused suspicion. These notes should be accurate and complete since it may be necessary to testify in court in the case at a later date. The documentation should include only factual information and not judgements or conclusions about the child or family members.

Often one hears concern expressed regarding the child welfare agency moving too slowly on the case. Due to heavy caseloads and reduced budget allocations, the child protection agency may be delayed in their investigations. The teacher should be patient and persist in referrals to the agency and/or person designated to accept responsibility for the case. Once the report and referral has been made, the school's task is not yet complete.

COUNSELING AND FOLLOW-UP

Until fairly recent times, the school's responsibilities terminated following their report to the child protection agency. Today, however, the school and its personnel must remain involved in the case to assist the child protection agency in their investigation and intervention in the suspected incestuous relationship. The school can then provide follow-up, support and counseling for the family unit as they assist child welfare in the case. The school typically has a relationship with the family prior to the initiation of the incestuous relationship and will continue its relationship with the family long after the child protection agency has closed its files on the case. The school can provide needed support and counseling for the child and family unit during the immediate crisis and work for the prevention of future incestuous behaviors. That supportive, cooperative relationship is critical to the welfare and development of the child within the school-community environment. The relationship between the school and family unit cannot and must not change nor terminate simply because report or referral for suspected sexual abuse/incest has been filed. Instead, the existing relationship expands to encompass new concerns (incest) and new personnel (community agencies involved in the intervention and treatment of incest). Therefore past supportive and cooperative relationships remain essentially in tact and more importantly unaltered in quality.

The school and its personnel should be careful not to make judgements concerning the child, parents or family regarding the suspected occurrence of incest. If school personnel suddenly withdraw or alter their relationship with the child or family, the result would no doubt be the projection of a judgemental attitude towards the family and would be detrimental to its recovery.

PREVENTION OF INCEST

The school can also play a significant role in the prevention of incestuous relationships. Prevention is often subdivided into three major categories: primary, secondary, and tertiary.

On a primary level, prevention of incest can occur through the provision of programs which improve familial relationships. Incest is an indication that family relationships and family function have broken down and need to be strengthened. Secondary prevention requires an intervention into families manifesting signs of child abuse/incest. Early intervention permits early treatment of factors contributing to incestuous behaviors.

Tertiary prevention necessitates treatment after incestuous relationships are substantiated. The treatment process may be long term, 2–3 years, be directed toward the family unit and individual family members and have as its goal the rehabilitation of the family and the prevention of any further victimization of the victims.[9]

More specifically, the school and its personnel have a role in all components of the prevention model:

1. Help create an awareness of the incest problem among the community in general and among other professionals.
2. Provide parent-teacher organization programs on child abuse/sexual abuse/incest.
3. Promote legislation on all levels for the detection, intervention, treatment and prevention of incest.
4. Provide training through inservice programs for lay persons and professionals pertaining to all aspects of the incest problem.
5. Serve as a coordinating group for various community services in providing for the well-being of incestuous families.
6. Develop and implement programs to follow-up on families who may move periodically or from area to area within the school system.
7. Implement comprehensive school health education, K–12. Many specific aspects of the sexual abuse/incest problem are addressed in health education areas such as: interpersonal relationships, mental and emotional health, stress, coping skills, family life education, personal health issues, community organizations, plus numerous others.

8. Provide programming which prepares one for parenthood, either as part of health education and/or as a separate curriculum offering.

SUMMARY

Most would agree that sexual abuse/incest is harmful to the family structure as well as individual family members. Numerous people have been traumatized, some irreparably, due to their involvement in an incestuous relationship. The school must become a leader in and advocate for a reduction in the incidence of sexual abuse/incest. The school presently has mechanisms for the detection, intervention and prevention of incestuous behavior. School personnel must assume their legal and, perhaps more importantly, moral responsibility to protect and promote the health and welfare of children. School personnel must be aware of the existence of incest, be cognizant of indicators, be observant for its detection, decide to become involved, report and follow-up on the report and be a support group for community agencies and the family. School personnel can make the difference. As it has been said, "If schools are not or will not be part of the solution, could they be part of the problem?"

REFERENCES

1. Forward S, Buck C: *Betrayal of Innocence: Incest and Its Devastation.* Los Angeles, JP Tarcher Inc, 1978.

2. Lustig N, Dresser JW, Spellman SE, et al: Incest. *Arch Gen Psychiat* 14: 31–40, 1966.

3. Justice B, Justice R: *The Broken Taboo: Sex in the Family.* New York, Human Sciences Press, 1979.

4. Rosenfeld AA, Nadelson CC, Krieger M, et al: Incest and sexual abuse of children. *J of Child Psychiatry* 16(2): 327–339, 1977.

5. Intra-family sexual abuse of children. Washington, National Center on Child Abuse and Neglect, 1976.

6. Giarretto H: The treatment of father-daughter incest: A psycho-social approach. *Child Today* 29(4):2–5, 34–35, 1976.

7. Sgroi SM: Introduction: A national needs assessment for protecting child victims of sexual assault, in *Sexual Assault of Children and Adolescents.* Burgess AW, Groth AN, Holmstrom LL, et al (eds). Lexington, Mass, Lexington Books, Chapter 1, 1978.

8. Weinberg, SK: *Incest Behavior.* Secaucus, New Jersey, Citadel Press, 1976.

9. Zaphiris AG: *Incest: The Family with Two Victims.* Englewood, Co., American Humane Association, 1978.

10. Woodbury J, Schwartz E: *The Silent Sin: A Case History of Incest.* New York, Signet Books, 1971.

11. Largen MA: Foreword, in *Sexual Assault of Children and Adolescents.* Burgess AW, Groth AN, Holstrom LL, et al (eds). Lexington, Mass., Lexington Books, 1978.

12. Streilein P: Social work professor attacks problems of sexually abused. *U of Houston Horizons* 1(5): 5, 1981.

13. Luther SL, Price JH: Child sexual abuse: A review. *J Sch Health* 50(3): 161–165, 1980.

14. Weeks R: The sexually exploited child. *Southern Med J* 69(7): 848–849, 1976.

15. Broadhurst DD: *The Educator's Role in the Prevention and Treatment of Child Abuse and Neglect.* Washington, National Center on Child Abuse and Neglect, 1979.

16. Baker S: Sexual abuse of children. Mendocino, Ca., Lawren Productions, 1978.

17. Tormes YM: *Child Victims of Incest.* Englewood, Co., American Humane Association, 1968.

18. *New Light on an Old Problem: 9 Questions and Answers About Child Abuse and Neglect.* Washington, National Center on Child Abuse and Neglect, 1978.

19. Leone DM: Sexual abuse of children. *AORN Journal* 27(4): 642–644, 1978.

20. *Interdisciplinary Glossary on Child Abuse and Neglect: Legal, Medical, Social Work Terms.* Washington, National Center on Child Abuse and Neglect, 1978.

21. Keller E (ED): Counseling the victim of sexual assault in *Sexual Assault: A Statewide Problem.* St. Paul, Minn., Minnesota Program for Victims of Sexual Assault, Chapter 3, 1974.

You Can Help a Sexually Abused Child

by Janet Rosenzweig

The sexual exploitation of children is a statistically startling fact of life. The National Center on Child Abuse and Neglect predicts that 20 out of every 100 children, both girls and boys, will be victimized in some manner before they reach their eighteenth birthday.

Statistics on sexual abuse are inexact, due in part to variations in the definition. Sexual abuse can include a wide range of behaviors, from fondling to rape, including juvenile prostitution and pornography. For practical purposes, and for explaining the issue to children, *sexual abuse can be described as being touched, looked at, or spoken to in ways that children feel is an invasion of their privacy.*

PROFILE OF AN ABUSED CHILD

How do you know that a child has been sexually abused? There is a myriad of signs and symptoms. While the appearance of any one symptom does not signify sexual abuse, the presence of several signs may indicate a possible victim.

The behavioral symptoms are similar to those associated with depression. Withdrawal or aggressive behavior may be noted. Self-destructive acts are often common among older children. These include substance abuse, self-mutilation, promiscuity, attempts to run away, and suicide threats or attempts. Younger children may exhibit a preoccupation with their own genitalia or those of other children. Many sexual abuse victims will refuse to dress for physical education

Janet Rosenzweig is Executive Director of the Girls Club of Dallas, Texas and a consultant to the Texas Department of Human Resources for sex abuse programs. "You Can Help a Sexually Abused Child" is reprinted from *Instructor,* April 1984, volume 93, pp. 62–64. Copyright © 1984 by the Instructor Publications, Inc. Used by permission.

classes, often fearing that there is something different or dirty about their bodies that others will notice.

Some sexual abuse victims may impose sex play on other children; however, the key word is *impose*. A mutual decision to engage in "you show me yours and I'll show you mine" is not necessarily problematic. However, should a child use force of any nature to secure the cooperation of another child, the act cannot be considered mutual and the instigator should be suspected of being a victim.

Children's art may also provide a clue. Drawings of adults displaying prominent genitalia and self-portraits indicating great isolation are two common signs.

Low self-esteem is typical in victims. They are implicitly taught that their value is for *what they do* (in this case, be a sex partner for an adult) as opposed to *who they are*. When they demonstrate such poor self-esteem, they may become the target for scapegoating by peers.

Sexual abuse victims have often been robbed of the chance to learn to make smart decisions concerning their own safety. For this reason, they may be revictimized in other circumstances.

WHEN A VICTIM CONFIDES IN YOU

A child will often try to communicate that something is wrong. This is extremely difficult for younger and older children alike; our culture gives young people the message that sex is not something they talk about with adults. In addition, they most likely have been told by the abuser not to tell. And, if incest is the problem, they are often dreadfully afraid of what will happen to their family when people find out. But many children will test the water with a trusted adult, possibly seeking an opinion on hypothetical problems. If you are the one a child confides in, there are several do's and don'ts to keep in mind.

Do believe the victim. A child rarely lies about sexual abuse, and even if he or she does, a need for professional help is still indicated. Not believing someone adds to the problem—most likely other people the child may have tried to talk to have not believed the child either. A child may seriously begin to doubt his or her own sanity when repeatedly told that what he or she knows to be true is not.

Do emphasize that the victim is not at fault. Often a child has been led to believe that he or she provoked the attack. Under no circumstances is a child victim ever considered at fault. Regardless of the child's appearance, manner of dress, or behavior, the adult must be responsible for his or her own behavior. Moreover, if a child is behaving in a precociously seductive fashion, someone must have encouraged and rewarded such behavior.

Do acknowledge the child's conflicts, which arise from several places. Primarily, the child is confused about the repercussions of the report, which will certainly cause a crisis for both victim and family, as the social and legal systems begin their intervention. A child may also have a conflict regarding feelings for the offender; in spite of the attack, there may be true affection for the offender. It is possible, and with male victims of female offenders often probable, that the victim experienced sexual arousal. Given that the sexual response system is a function of the autonomic nervous system and a reflect response to stimulus, the child may be terribly confused about something that in some way felt good, even though he or she is sure it was wrong. An analogy to laughing when tickled, or getting goose bumps when cold, can be understood by a child.

Do not ever make a promise to a child that you cannot keep. Victims have most likely been lied to by adults in the past. They need to learn to trust adults again. A common temptation is to let a child talk you into promising not to tell anyone. This explicitly removes your ability to take control of the situation. Relinquishing control to responsible adults is a vital step in the healing process of the victim. Of course, it is also illegal to fail to report child abuse of any type to local child protective services authorities. Explain to the child that you want to find a special person to help him or her, someone with the child's best interests at heart, someone who understands sexual abuse problems.

Do know the resources in your community. Every state has a Child Protective Service Unit, located within a larger state agency. Many Child Protective Service Units even have specially trained sexual abuse case workers. Local police and sheriff departments and some hospitals have either specialized child abuse or sex crime teams. Many family service agencies provide treatment for victims and their families, as may your local mental health agency. It would be good to call these agencies and learn who the specialists are before you need to contact them. An agency might also provide speakers at faculty meetings on identifying and helping victims.

Do not ever ask an incest victim why he or she let it go on so long. Data from different treatment programs indicate that the incest may have been going on from several months to several years before a report is made. By asking why a victim let it go on so long, you are implying that the child had the ability to stop it.

Do cooperate with Child Protective Service workers. They will often want to interview the child at school. Unless the first contact with the child is away from parents, he or she may defer and retract the allegations in their presence. Protect the child's confidentiality; have him or her called to the school nurse or counselor's office as if nothing is particularly out of the ordinary. If a child's protection will be best served by removal from home, make lessons and homework available. A child often loses ground in schoolwork while in protective custody.

Do be as supportive as you can be to a victim seeking help. It is truly difficult to take that first step. It is our job as caring adults to make that first step as rewarding as possible.

PROGRAMS AND RESOURCES

Programs designed to help prevent sexual abuse generally incorporate many of the basic health education principles. The goals of prevention programs are to teach children that their bodies belong to them, that they need to learn to make good decisions about them, and that there are people who can help them do this. The American Cancer Society's "Early Start to Good Health" curriculum may be used to introduce these points to young children.

The Illusion Theater in Minneapolis has pioneered the idea of the touch continuum; there is good touch and bad touch and children can sense the difference. Learning that they do not have to accept the bad touching is important. Parents should let children make their own decisions about whom to touch, and should be discouraged from forcing a child to hug or kiss people if the child does not want to.

Staff from local sexual abuse programs will often be available to present special programs in the classroom or in special assemblies. Often after a sensitively done program on sexual abuse, victims will identify themselves to the speaker or their teacher. Be prepared for this. It is important to know in advance exactly how you need to proceed in your community.

Child sexual abuse is a serious and complex problem, requiring input from all community systems concerned with the welfare of children and their families. Schools can play a vital role by directing child victims to help, and by implementing prevention programs.

The following groups and centers will provide information or materials to help you develop your own prevention program.

Bubbylonian Encounter (film): National Committee for Prevention of Child Abuse—Kansas Chapter, Suite 301, 214 W. 6th St., Topeka, KS 66603. See INSTRUCTOR, January 1984, p. 26.

Child Abuse and Neglect: A Teacher's Handbook for Detection, Reporting, and Classroom Management ($7.95 in paperback, $14.95 hardbound); NEA Professional Library, PO Box 509, West Haven, CT 06516. A companion leaflet. "What Parents Should Know about Child Sexual Abuse," is available in packages of 25 for $4.95 from the same address.

Child Sexual Abuse Prevention Project, a guidebook for developing a curriculum for children, created by Illusion Theater. For complete information, write: Sexual Assault Services, Hennepin County Attorney's Office, C-2000 Government Center, Minneapolis, MN 55487. Cost is $8 including postage. Other resources such as posters and study cards are also available.

Come Tell Me Right Away (booklet); Edupress, Inc., PO Box 583, Fayetteville, NY 13066. Cost: $2.50.

Dangerous Stranger, 11-minute videotape for elementary children. Available free except for small cost of dubbing the video on the videotape you provide. For information write: Charles F. Ash, Jr., Pennsylvania State Police, U.S. 422, Limerick, PA 19468.

Some Secrets Should Be Told, conversation with puppets on sexual abuse, geared to grades K–6. Developed by Massachusetts Society for the Prevention of Cruelty to Children. Can be purchased as a 10-minute film or as a filmstrip; a video version can be rented. For prices and further information contact: Family Information Systems, 69 Clinton Rd., Brookline, MA 02146.

What Everyone Should Know about Sexual Abuse of Children (100 pamphlets for $39); Channing L. Bete Co., Inc., 200 State Rd., South Deerfield, MA 01373.

Sexually Abused Children: Identification and Suggestions for Intervention

by Marla R. Brassard, Ann Tyler,
and Thomas J. Kehle

One of the most difficult problems that a school psychologist must deal with is the identification and treatment of school-aged victims of sexual abuse. Sex, particularly when it is intrafamilial or involves pre-adolescent children, is not a topic most school psychologists feel comfortable discussing with children. If lacking knowledge of how to identify and skillfully interview sexually abused children, school psychologists are unlikely to make appropriate referrals, and opportunities to help are impeded. This article is designed to help school psychologists: (a) identify victims of child abuse; (b) interview a victim and the victim's parents; (c) know who to notify when sexual abuse is suspected; and (d) identify suggested intervention and treatment approaches that are appropriate in the practice of school psychology.

Child sexual abuse has been defined as "any contact or interaction between a child and an adult in which the child is being used for the sexual stimulation of the perpetrator or another person" (Broadhurst, 1979, p. 152). The child may be requested to be a participant, recipient, or observer of inappropriate sexual behavior. "Sexual abuse may also be committed by a person under the age of 18 when that person is either significantly older than the victim or

Marla R. Brassard is a member of the faculty, Department of Educational Psychology, University of Georgia. She is co-author of this article with Ann Tyler and Thomas J. Kehle. "Sexually Abused Children: Identification and Suggestions for Intervention" is reprinted from *School Psychology Review,* National Association of School Psychologists, 1983, volume 12, number 1, pp. 93–96. Reprinted by permission of the publisher.

when the perpetrator is in a position of power or control over another child" (Broadhurst, 1979, p. 152).

Most reported cases of child abuse involve young female children and their male guardians, older male relatives, or other older males that they know. Females are reported victims in 10 times as many cases as males (DeFrancis, 1969; DeVine, 1980). In 97% of the cases reported the offenders are male; 50 to 80% of child sexual abuse victims are abused by people they know; and parents and other relatives account for 30 to 50% of the reported cases (DeFrancis, 1969; McGeorge, 1955; Sgroi, 1975). That the percentage of intrafamilial abuse is in actuality higher is suggested by the fact that children are more likely to report abuse when it involves a stranger than when it involves a parent (DeFrancis, 1969; Landis, 1956). The average age of female victims, in studies of victims under the age of 16, was 11, although cases ranged from infancy to early adulthood (DeFrancis, 1969). More recent data (American Humane Society, 1981) reports that 72% of incest victims are 13 years or older.

When sexual abuse is discovered, the already detrimental exploitative adult-child relationship is exacerbated. The victim often perceives herself (Note 1) as a betrayer of the family and responsible for the breakup of her support system. This often includes alienation from her mother, denial or hostility from her father, and suspiciousness from her siblings. The abused child may react with denial, hostility toward both parents, or compliance. The long term effects of sexual abuse are not clearly known. Some children appear to have lasting psychological problems, and there is evidence that intrafamilial abuse may be passed from one generation to another (Raphling, Carpenter, & Davis, 1967; American Humane Society, 1981). In addition, correlational studies indicate the following (Kroth, 1979, p. 99):

1. 70% of adolescent drug addicts were involved in some form of family sexual abuse.
2. 75% of adolescent prostitutes have been involved in incestuous relationships.
3. Sexual abuse has been identified as one of the three main reasons why children run away from home.
4. 50% of the children in a reformatory in Maine and nearly all the children in a Chicago reformatory had been sexually molested prior to commitment.

In contrast, other sexually abused children may be quite able to cope, particularly if abuse is by a same generational partner such as a brother.

In the school setting, sexual abuse is usually discovered when: (a) a child is referred for inappropriate sex play with other children, or (b) a child confides in a teacher or other trusted professional that she has been sexually molested by a caretaker. In addition, there are some physical and behavioral signs that school psychologists and/or school nurses should be alert for. These include:

1. Difficulty in walking or sitting.
2. Torn, stained, or bloody underclothing.
3. Complaints of pain or itching in the genital area.
4. Bruises or bleeding in external genitalia, vaginal or anal area.
5. Venereal disease, particularly in a child under 13.
6. Poor peer relationships.
7. Behavior typical of a younger child such as bedwetting or infantile, withdrawn or even retarded behavior.
8. A change in appetite or sleeping patterns.
9. Need for an unusual degree of reassurance from a parent and excessive clinging, particularly when the offender is around.
10. Unwillingness to change for gym or participate in physical activities.
11. Fear and anxiety regarding the opposite sex.
12. Bizarre, sophisticated, or unusual sexual knowledge or behavior.
13. Indiscriminate hugging, kissing, or seductive behavior with children or adults.

The effects of child abuse frequently appear to be symptoms of other problems. For example, in one case a 5 year old kindergarten child was referred to us for what initially appeared to be a school phobia. After a relatively successful adjustment to her kindergarten class in the fall, she suddenly refused to attend school. The teacher and the mother reported that they were forced to ". . .chase her around the stationwagon, catch her, and drag her into the classroom each morning." The obvious intervention appeared to be behavioral desensitization. However, after the parent intake interview and a review of the child's recent medical history, it was discovered that following an uncle's Thanksgiving visit, she became ill and required treatment for a vaginal infection. A subsequent parent interview revealed that the mother was suspicious about her brother's possible sexual behavior toward the child. The child was then interviewed in the presence of the mother and the kindergarten teacher. Relevant questions confirmed that the uncle had sexually molested the child. Consequently, it was our interpretation that the child was not necessarily school phobic, but was afraid of leaving the protection of her parents. Having the kindergarten teacher and mother present during the interview encouraged a supportive and sympathetic atmosphere both in the home and the school setting and served to reassure the child that these individuals would protect her from incidents of abuse. This "mini-therapy," along with instructions to the child on how to say no to inappropriate touch and report it to her parents, aided in the child's understanding of the incident and consequently the child's readjustment to the classroom environment.

Adolescents may respond to abuse in a number of different ways. For example, they may engage in delinquency or run away; play a parenting, central role in the family; or exhibit suicidal behavior and/or depression.

If abuse is strongly suspected on the basis of physical and behavioral signs, the case should be referred to the county child protection unit. In some cases it may be necessary for the school psychologist, if he or she has the skills to do so, to interview the child further. Whenever possible, however, school personnel should allow trained personnel from a child abuse agency to handle interviews or manage them jointly.

When children are referred or approach an adult to discuss sexual abuse, they are often apprehensive about the consequences of reporting to someone and are embarrassed about discussing the subject of sex. Obviously, they need to be made as comfortable as possible in the interview situation. With adolescents, the suspicion of abuse should be followed by inquiry. If abuse has occurred, the victim is generally relieved by the opportunity to share the "secret" with a professional. The younger child may give clues to possible abuse in her drawings of family and self, in her play with anatomically correct dolls, or in her doll house play. All such signs should be followed with appropriate questioning. Some suggestions for the interview are:

1. Conduct the interview in a private setting.
2. Maintain an atmosphere of informality and trust.
3. If it becomes apparent on the basis of information obtained during the interview that abuse has occurred and consequently a report will be made, the child should receive a clear and understandable reason of why such reporting is necessary.
4. Be sensitive to the child's nonverbal cues, in addition to employing language that is clearly comprehensible to the child. Conversely, if words or expressions used by the child are ambiguous, ask for clarification.
5. Believe the child; children rarely lie about sexual abuse.
6. Reassure the child that she has done nothing wrong and that she will have your continuing support.
7. Do not suggest answers to the child, and avoid probing or pressing for answers.
8. Do not display horror, shock, or disapproval of parents, child, or situation.

9. Do not ask or suggest to the child that the interview should be concealed from the parents.
10. If possible, record the interview and inform the child of such.

If an interview with the parents is necessary, focus the discussion on the best interests of the child. Again, in most cases, it is more appropriate for the child protection agency to interview parents. Obviously, the parents will be emotionally upset. The mother may react with guilt, resulting from her perceived negligence. She may, in addition, focus the discussion on her anger at the offender. If the offender is the father, he may deny the abuse or challenge the veracity of the accuser. The interview should not broach the topic of separation or removal of family members. Specifically, the parent interview should possess and/or stress the following (Broadhurst, 1979):

1. Be direct regarding the purpose of the interview.
2. Conduct the interview in a private setting.
3. Reassure the parents of the support of yourself and the school.
4. Clearly inform the parents if the abuse or suspected abuse will be reported. Advise the parents of the school's legal responsibility.
5. Do not attempt to "prove" abuse.
6. Do not display anger or disapproval of the parent(s), child, or situation. Do not imply blame or make judgments about the parents or child.

School psychologists should be familiar with the state laws on reporting child abuse. All states have laws regarding abuse; most states require educators, including teachers, administrators, and pupil personnel staff in any public or private school, to report. Failure to do so results in a Class B misdemeanor for the negligent party. Where to report varies from state to state but usually involves some agency such as the Child Protective Services and a Division of Family Services. No state requires proof of abuse, only a statement about the condition of the child. Oral reporting is usually required immediately upon suspicion of abuse. Written reporting is usually required within one or two days. Every state provides immunity from civil liability and/or criminal penalty for those who do report, provided the report is made in good faith.

Generally, school districts have their own policy or are in the process of developing policies on reporting cases of sexual abuse and neglect. District policies function to inform personnel of their responsibilities and provide administrative support for those who actually do the reporting. School psychologists can play a central role in establishing policy if it does not exist. They can also be instrumental in ensuring that administrators and other school personnel are aware of the policy and relevant state laws.

There are several common difficulties that arise in schools and serve to impede reporting. School personnel often state that they do not want to become involved or that they do not want to jeopardize a relationship with a family by reporting abuse. School principals sometimes discourage staff reporting or do not follow through once a case has been reported to them. Similar problems are evident with central office administrators. Again, as is true in the case of some individual school psychologists, district administrators may feel uncomfortable with the topic of sexual abuse. School personnel must be aware that not reporting cases of sexual abuse can result in civil prosecution of the individual(s) who knew of the abuse but did not report it. The civil action can be brought by the offender against school personnel who neglected to report the abuse. School psychologists can function to inform school personnel, via workshops and in-service sessions, alleviating many of the difficulties regarding reporting.

Helping parents locate resources available in most communities may be the most valuable intervention that the school psychologist is able to employ. One excellent referral source is *Parents United* (Note 2) which offers group treatment by and for child abusers. Another form of support service is "crisis nurseries" (Note 3) which offer temporary shelter for abused children as well as places for parents in crisis to leave their children until the crisis abates (usually within a couple of days). In addition to the protective and caretaker aspects of the crisis nursery, such centers may provide family and individual therapy for parents and teenage victims of abuse.

It should be stressed that many school psychologists do not possess the expertise or experience to deal effectively with the problem of sexual abuse. In these cases the most realistic intervention is an intelligent referral. The reporting of the abuse and suggestions to the parents regarding referral are perhaps the first steps in stopping the sexual mistreatment of the child. Working cooperatively with a referral agency increases the support system of the child.

There are a few intervention techniques that have been established for dealing with sexual abuse. With adolescent children, group techniques as employed in *Daughters and Sons United* (Note 2), have been effective in decreasing social isolation and reestablishing a sense of self-control and self-respect. There are also preventive programs available such as *You're in Charge* (Note 4) which in a play-form teaches children that they have control over their bodies and they have the right to say "no" to anyone who touches them inappropriately. Preventive programs function to educate the child about what is appropriate and inappropriate contact between children and adults.

In summary, school psychologists often occupy a unique liaison role which can function to enhance home-school-agency intervention efforts. Being able to identify probable sexual abuse, reporting it to the appropriate agency, and subsequently working in concert with the agency, increases the likelihood of stopping the abuse and helping the child to overcome the often detrimental effects of abuse.

REFERENCE NOTES

1. Because of the documented preponderence of female victims and male perpetrators, victims are referred to in the article as "she" or "her" and perpetrators as "he" or "him."

2. For complete information regarding *Parents United* and *Daughters and Sons United* contact: Harry Giaretto, Ph.D., Director, *Help for Sexually Abused Children and Their Families,* Parents United National Headquarters, P.O. Box 952, San Jose, CA 95108.

3. Developed by Ann Tyler at the Family Support Center of Salt Lake City, Utah. Requests for further information regarding the *Crisis Nursery* should be sent to Ann Tyler, Family Support Center, 2020 Lake Street, Salt Lake City, Utah 84105.

4. For complete information contact: Darly Barrett or Susan Cameron, *You're in Charge,* P.O. Box 1344, Freeport Center, Clearfield, Utah 84106.

REFERENCES

American Humane Association. Sexual abuse of children. AHA, 1981.

Broadhurst, D. *The educators role in the prevention and treatment of child abuse and neglect.* U.S. Department of Health, Education and Welfare. DHEW Publication No. (OHDS) 79-30172, August, 1979.

DeFrancis, V. *Protecting the child victim of sex crimes committed by adults, final report.* Denver: American Humane Association. Children's Division, 1969.

Devine, R.A. Incest: a review of the literature, in *Sexual abuse of children: selected readings.* U.S. Department of Health and Human Services, DHHS Publication No. (OHDS) 78-30161, November, 1980.

Kroth, J.A. *Child sexual abuse* Springfield, IL: Charles Humas, 1979.

Landis, J.T. Experiences of 500 children with adult sexual deviation. *Psychiatric Quarterly Supplement,* 1956, *30,* 91–109.

MacFarlane, K. Sexual abuse of children in Chapman, J.R. & Gates, M. (Eds.) *The victimization of women,* Sage Yearbooks in Women's Policy Studies, Beverly Hills/London: Sage Publications, Inc., 1978, *3,* 81–109.

McGeorge, J. Sexual assaults on children. *Medicine, science, and law,* 1955, *4,* 245–253.

Raphling, D.L., Carpenter, B.L., Davis, A. Incest: A geneological study. *Archives of General Psychiatry,* 1967, *16,* 505–511.

Sgroi, S.M. Sexual molestation of children: the last frontier in child abuse. *Children Today,* 1975, *4,* 19–44.

The Play Technique: Diagnosing the Sexually Abused Child

by Ann French Clark and Jane Bingham

Though sex seems always to be in the media, the fact remains that for most of us sex is a topic that remains if not taboo, at least slightly inhibiting. Parents and others in charge of children spend a great deal of time trying to govern what their child will ask about and what their child will say. Naturally, this is appropriate to ensure that children grow into socially acceptable adults. However, the very fact that children are admonished by many that sex is dirty, that they shouldn't talk about it, etc., is what makes it easy for the offender to have a ready victim.

It is more difficult to get the child to reveal an incident involving sexual contact. This difficulty in talking about a problematic subject is a bane to professionals working with children. Adults often fail to realize what skills are necessary to find out information from children. Commonly, children are treated as miniature adults with all the attendant expectations. It is no wonder that those who have this approach fail.

Talking to children is easy as long as one remembers that a child's field of knowledge is not as great as that of an adult. Therefore, it only follows that adults should use the language of children. The adult must be cognizant of child development and must mesh expectations to a child's ability.

In the area of child sexual abuse it is disconcerting to adults when children use graphic words and gestures to illustrate what has

Ann French Clark is Supervisor of the Sexual Abuse Investigation Unit, Texas Department of Human Services, Ft. Worth, Texas. She is co-author with Jane Bingham, Educational Coordinator of the Multidisciplinary Institute for Child Sexual Abuse Intervention and Treatment. "The Play Technique: Diagnosing the Sexually Abused Child" is reprinted from *Tarrant County Physician*, August 1984. Reprinted by permission of the authors.

happened to them. This conflict of child language versus adult sexual functions can alarm the unprepared adult.

IMPLICATIONS IN SEXUAL ABUSE CASES

Preschool

The preschooler will be able to:

1. show what happened, using dolls or play materials
2. say who did it
3. tell if it hurt
4. tell what the person said to them

The preschooler will be unable to:

1. give a time or date when an event happened
2. give a complete narrative account of incident
3. understand implications of revealing sensitive information

Behaviors that may result from sexual abuse at this age:

1. regression, which may take the form of loss of toilet training, baby talk
2. night terrors, fears
3. clinging behavior
4. curiosity and outgoing behavior may be squelched
5. child may act out at an older age, due to the ability to suppress now

It is easier to repress traumatic events at this age, than at any other.

The School Age Child (6–11)

The school age child will be able to:

1. give a detailed account of what happened
2. may or may not use dolls or play materials to assist
3. say who did it
4. tell in general terms when incident happened (e.g.: when I was in the 3rd grade, during daytime, near Christmas)
5. tell where incident happened
6. tell duration of abuse (e.g.: since I was four years old)
7. tell first and last times incident happened
8. understand some implications of revealing "the secret"

More likely at this age to tell a friend, or a friend's mother.
The school age child will be unable to:

1. give exact dates of incident
2. understand why he/she is not to blame
3. suppress the incident as readily as a younger child

Behaviors that may result from sexual abuse at this age:

1. bedwetting, thumb sucking or other forms of regression
2. early or late to school
3. tantrums
4. pseudo-adult behavior
5. marked interest in sex
6. changes in grades, other behaviors

The Adolescent

The adolescent will be able to:

1. tell exactly what happened
2. say when, how, where, duration, etc.
3. understand all implications of revealing the secret
4. may or may not be a "good" witness

The adolescent will be unable to:

1. understand why this happened
2. forgive the mother who is most often seen as contributing to
   what has happened

This age child is more likely to feel extreme guilt and responsibility, and be less concerned with getting in trouble.
Behaviors that may result from sexual abuse at this age:

1. extreme loss of self-esteem
2. promiscuity
3. run away
4. moody, depressed, crying jags
5. poor school performance
6. drop out of school
7. drop friends of long standing
8. sudden change in values, etc.
9. overly compliant
10. too many responsibilities for age
11. will have very little free time for extracurricular activities
12. behavioral regression
13. drug and alcohol abuse

AIDS TO COMMUNICATION

Dolls

Dolls may be used with any age child who is comfortable with them. Many feel they are most appropriate with preschool and early school age. However, it has been the experience in Tarrant County, through hundreds of videotaped interviews of child abuse victims, that this is not always the case. Preschoolers lacking inhibitions often prefer to use their own bodies to describe where they were touched. They may also interact with the dolls as if they are actual people. The dolls themselves are an abstraction to this preschool age in that they have problems understanding what the interviewer expects of them.

For example, a caseworker or Rape Crisis volunteer might say to the child, "Show me where he touched you" meaning for the child to use the doll as themselves. The child may not grasp that concept, preferring instead to point to or touch their own body.

Anatomical Drawings

Anatomical drawings can be very helpful when used in the investigation and intervention of child sexual abuse. One resource, containing 32 line drawings of front and back views of white and black males and females at four chronological phases of development, is available from Forensic Mental Health Association.

After rapport is established, the drawings can be introduced as an activity to clarify or document what is being said. The child can pick out the drawing that best represents him/her and the perpetrator. The child can draw a circle around specific body parts indicated in the story and the victim's descriptive words can be used as labels. It may be necessary to sketch on clothing if the victim and perpetrator were not completely undressed.

Avoid terms such as "let's pretend" so that the investigation will be seen as valid rather than play. Asking whether or not the child has seen people undressed like this before helps to determine the use of pornography. The drawings can also be cut out for paper dolls as an alternative tool for interviewing.

Some children may shy away from exposure to the drawings, not from discomfort, but as a result of an experienced trauma they associate with what they are viewing. This reaction should be documented as clinical evidence of a sexually traumatized child.

The drawings may prove to be more comfortable for male victims than play with dolls. Also, drawing and coloring are not as sex role specific as doll play.

Puzzles, Puppets, Doll Houses, Paperdolls

Toys which are readily available such as paperdolls, puppets, puzzles, and doll houses are aids to interviewing children who have been abused. The professional can ascertain where the abuse happened and often how it effected the child. As always, the adult should remember that being on the child's level will help facilitate rapport and communications.

Art

Children express themselves effectively through the art medium. Underlying emotional problems may surface in free art more than in a structured conversational interview. Dr. Suzanne Sgroi often uses art as a tool in her private pediatric practice. One technique is to ask the child to draw a picture of themselves or of their family.

Children who have been abused often have poor self concepts and distorted body images. Those who are abused sexually may not realize they are conveying through art when they draw exaggerated or missing genitalia. The professional person can elicit further explanations by asking the child "to tell me about your picture." The child's comments should be written on the artwork which can be retained in the medical or social work file. It is a common mistake for professionals to send the art home with the children, thus destroying any chance for future therapeutic intervention.

CONCLUSION

It is very important that all physicians remember that they may be the first person, and perhaps the only one, to suspect, or know of, sexual abuse of a child. To have to admit such silent violence exists in this society increases the responsibility of protection for children.

Children are victimized at an astounding rate. In 1983, the Texas Department of Human Resources confirmed 6,079 reported cases of child sexual abuse in this state, alone. It is mandatory to report suspected cases so an investigation can be done (Family Code, Chapter 34.01).

All children need to be reassured at the time of outcry by being told they are believed. One can also tell the child help is available to stop the abusive situation.

Doctors may be reassured to know that a confirmed case of child sexual abuse makes a break in the cycle of violence which helps prevent future victimization. Please help us reduce this risk for all our children.

BIBLIOGRAPHY

Clark, Ann. *Ages and Stages in Child Sexual Abuse.* Children Who Wait Conference, 1983, 1984.

Groth, A. Nicholas, and Birnbaum, H. Jean. *Men Who Rape: The Psychology of the Offender.* Plenum Press, New York, 1979.

Groth, A. Nicholas, and Stevenson, Thomas M. *Anatomical Drawings.* Forensic Mental Health Associates, 3 Ireland Road, Newton Center, MA 02159.

Harnest, June. *Teach-A Bodies.* Copyright, 1983.

Sgroi, Suzanne M. *A Handbook of Clinical Intervention in Child Sexual Abuse.* Lexington Books, Lexington, Mass. 1982.

The Testimony of the Child Victim of Sexual Assault

by Lucy Berliner and Mary Kay Barbieri

Sexual abuse of children, though widely condemned, is nevertheless more prevalent than has been previously realized. When the accused offender does not admit guilt, the testimony of the child victim is likely to be the only or the main evidence. Members of the criminal-justice system often share general societal beliefs that children are not as credible as adults and that children cannot participate in such legal proceedings without serious trauma. In this article, we address some of the social and legal barriers to successful prosecution of child sexual abuse cases, and to the child's effective participation in such cases. Then, we discuss some steps that can be taken to help reduce, eliminate, or overcome these barriers.

Prosecution of child sexual assault often rests largely on the child victim's testimony. Yet there are both social and legal barriers to the acceptance of the child's statements as courtroom evidence. Furthermore, court appearance under such potentially traumatic circumstances can pose some psychological hazards for the child. But, we feel, these barriers and hazards are not insurmountable. Between us, we have had direct experience with hundreds of cases of child sexual assault, as a social worker in a specialty clinic that treats child victims and as an attorney in the prosecutor's office, respectively. On

Lucy Berliner practices at the Sexual Assault Center, Harborview Medical Center, Seattle, Washington. Mary Kay Barbieri was Deputy Prosecuting Attorney for the city of Seattle, Washington and is currently a member of the staff of the University of Puget Sound Law School. "The Testimony of the Child Victim of Sexual Assault" is reprinted from *Journal of Social Issues,* 1984, volume 40, number 2, pp. 125–137. Copyright © 1984 by Plenium Publishing Corporation. Reprinted by permission of the publisher.
Author's Note: We would like to thank Joseph McGrath for this thoughtful editing of an earlier draft of this paper. Correspondence concerning this article should be addressed to Lucy Berliner, Sexual Assault Center, Harborview Medical Center, 325 Ninth Avenue, Seattle, WA 98104.

the basis of that experience, we will argue in this paper that both the potential psychological hazards to the child, and the social and legal barriers to effective courtroom performance by the child can be overcome, circumvented, or eliminated if the adults involved in the criminal-justice process take certain appropriate steps to deal with them. This paper is about those hazards and barriers, and about the steps we think can be taken to deal with them.

THE NATURE OF THE PROBLEM

Sexual activity with children is prohibited by custom in all known societies and is illegal in every state of this country (Herman, 1981), regardless of the degree or type of coercion by the adult, or accommodation by the victim. Children under a certain age are considered legally incapable of consenting to sexual relations. Although there are a few exceptions to this generalization at certain times and in certain cultures these typically occur only under strictly defined cultural circumstances (such as during a puberty rite). The crime has been known as rape, statutory rape, indecent assault, incest, sexual battery, criminal sexual conduct, indecent liberties, and a variety of other names (Bulkley, 1981a). By whatever name, child molestation is universally considered to be deviant behavior.

Yet it has been estimated that thousands of children are sexually victimized each year (Sarafino, 1979). Child sexual abuse can be generally defined as sexual contact with the child by an adult, by a person who is more than five years older than the child, or by anyone with the use of force. In retrospective studies of nonclinical adult populations, sexual abuse during childhood is reported by substantial percentages of respondents. For example, in one well-designed study of females in randomly selected households in a large western city, 38% reported having been sexually abused before age 18 (Russell, 1982). In another survey of college students, 19% of the women and 9% of the men reported having been victims of sexual abuse (Finkelhor, 1979). In both of those studies, most respondents said they did not report the assault(s) at the time.

In studies of clinical populations of molested children, most reported having been assaulted by a known and trusted adult, who used indirect or nonviolent means of coercion to involve them in repeated sexual activity (Conte & Berliner, 1981). Strangers constitute only a small percentage of offenders. Incest, once considered rare, is now believed to be a common type of child abuse. Parents and parent surrogates account for a substantial portion of offenders in reported cases (Burgess, Groth, Holmstrom, & Sgroi, 1978).

The offender often evades being caught by threatening or pressuring the child not to tell for fear of negative consequences. The child is usually no match for the adult in size, power, or sophistication, so the offender can often control and abuse the child over long periods of time without detection. If the child does report the abuse, the offender often denies it—and often is believed.

In addition to these features of child sexual abuse, which tend to keep offenders from being detected and prosecuted, there are a number of further barriers to successful prosecution of such cases once they are reported. There are four main reasons why it is so difficult to prosecute cases of sexual assault against children. First, adults are often skeptical when children report having been molested. Second, many lay and professional people believe that sexual abuse is caused by a mental disorder, and therefore that the mental-health system, not the criminal-justice system, is the proper forum for dealing with the matter. Third, many fear that children will be traumatized by taking part in such legal proceedings and hence be further victimized. Fourth, many prosecutors do not want to undertake cases that rest heavily on testimony of child victims because they fear that the child will not be able to perform adequately as a witness.

Can Children Be Believed as Witnesses?

The child's believability in sexual-assault cases arises first in relation to the parents or other adults in whom the child confides about the abuse, then in relation to doctors and counselors who treat the child, and later in relation to prosecutors, judges, juries, and others in the justice system. In the legal arena, the child's statements become official testimony. Therefore, a key issue is whether the child is judged to be competent to testify, and whether that testimony is credible.

While adults are often skeptical when children report sexual abuse, especially by those in or close to the family, there is little or no evidence indicating that children's reports are unreliable, and none at all to support the fear that children often make false accusations of sexual assault or misunderstand innocent behavior by adults. The general veracity of children's reports is supported by relatively high rates of admission by the offenders (Conte & Berliner, 1981). Not a single study has ever found false accusations of sexual assault a plausible interpretation of a substantial portion of cases (Burgess et al., 1978).

Recall that Freud originally contended that childhood sexual trauma formed the basis of his female patients' neuroses. He then altered that view, making his patients' *fantasies* of childhood sexual activity the cornerstone of his theoretical system. Some contend that he made the shift at least in part because it was personally and/or professionally more acceptable to disbelieve his patients than to accept the reality of widespread sexual abuse of children (Masson, 1984; Rush, 1977). It was after this shift that Freud's views became accepted by the medical/psychiatric community.

Our clinical experience indicates that many children who report being assaulted actually underreport the amount and type of abuse; exaggeration is rare. Moreover, children often fail to report, or recant their reports, because the consequences of telling seem even worse than the consequences of being victimized again (Gentry, 1978). But children can and do report such abuse if there is a climate of belief, as evidenced by the high rates of reporting in communities that have visible treatment programs for sexually abused children (Kroth, 1979). And those high rates of reporting are *not* accompanied by any evidence that such a climate has spawned an increase in "false positives."

Should Child Sexual Abusers Be Prosecuted or Rehabilitated?

Most child sexual abusers know that they are breaking the law and can be held legally responsible (Groth & Birnbaum, 1979). But many mental-health professionals believe that such offenders have psychological disorders that, in some sense, excuse their behavior and make them candidates for mental-health intervention. The family and the victim often share this goal of getting help for the offender, especially when the offender is in or known to the family. And from this viewpoint, the criminal-justice system offers only a punitive outcome.

But sexual offenders rarely seek mental-health treatment voluntarily. Some form of external pressure is almost always necessary to make them enter and complete treatment programs. Often, the law can be used effectively as a leverage, even when the goal of all concerned is treatment rather than punishment (Bulkley, 1981b).

Will the Child as Witness Suffer More Than the Child as Victim?

One major barrier to prosecution of child sexual-assault cases is the fear that the child will be further traumatized by involvement in the legal process. In cases where the accused is a stranger, children are more likely to be believed by the adults in their families, and the behavior is more likely to be viewed as criminal. But even under these circumstances, the victims and their families may be reluctant to report the crime to authorities because of the fear that the child will be subjected to further trauma by the criminal-justice process. It can be lengthy and requires the child to repeatedly face traumatic memories: The victims and their families can have no guarantee that the child will not encounter untrained or insensitive personnel.

When the offender is known to the family, there is an additional reluctance to report the crime or to follow up its prosecution, lest the victim or the offender be further injured. The most reluctance occurs when the offender is a family member. Many people hold greater loyalty to family members, even errant ones, than to society at large. Criminal prosecution of a family member, particularly a parent, is likely to have negative consequences for all family members. Furthermore, the child victim may have mixed feelings toward the accused. The child wants the abuse to stop but does not understand the necessity of legal intervention to stop it. The nonoffending parent, as well as the child, may feel dependent on the offender. On top of all these concerns, the child is likely to suffer guilt over accusing a family member of such a taboo crime, and fear hostility from and rejection by others in the family.

Will the Child Be a Credible Witness?

Prosecutors are reluctant to try a case that hinges mainly on the uncorroborated testimony of a child victim. Sexual abuse is a crime that by its very nature contains major burden-of-proof problems. There seldom are other witnesses or corroborating physical evidence. For the case to be successfully prosecuted, the child's competence must first be established; then, the child's statements, elicited under constraints defined by the formal structure of the law, must be believed. Furthermore, the crime usually involves many separate acts occurring over a period of time which are not reported until some much later time. In such circumstances, accurate reporting of the sequence of events is a difficult task for child or adult.

While these are difficult circumstances for obtaining accurate testimony, there is no reason to dismiss such testimony out of hand simply because of the age of the witness. To be sure, age differences in perceptual, memory, and verbal capacities should be taken into consideration in assessing witness competence. But research evidence (see Johnson & Foley, 1984; Marin, Holmes, Guth, & Kovac, 1979; Perlmutter, 1980) and our own practical experience suggest that children, even very young ones, can give valuable testimony if they are properly prepared for their courtroom appearances.

PROSECUTING CHILD SEXUAL ASSAULT CASES

Some communities have developed highly successful programs for the legal handling of child sexual-assault cases. These programs invariably seem to involve several key features. First, they are staffed by professionals who have been trained in several pertinent areas: the dynamics of child sexual assault; principles of child development, including emotional reactions such as fear, self-blame, and ambivalence; and interviewing and rapport-building techniques. Second, the intervention process of the criminal-justice system is modified in various ways to accommodate child witnesses: The investigation is telescoped to reduce the number of times the child is interviewed and the number of different people involved in those interviews. Sometimes joint inteviews are conducted, or videotaping used to reduce the need for repeat interviews. Third, the various steps are taken to make the child less anxious and more comfortable. Assigning the same people to handle the case all the way through the proceedings can help give the child the comfort of being with familiar adults. Special settings, such as playrooms, can help too. So can the use of interviewing aids, such as anatomically correct dolls, that permit the child to demonstrate the sexual activity rather than having to describe it verbally. These three features—professional personnel appropriately trained, a criminal-justice system that accommodates its procedures to the needs and capabilities of the child victim/witness, and a set of procedures designed to give support and comfort to the child—seem to be highly facilitative (if not necessary and sufficient) conditions for effective use of child witnesses in sexual assault cases. They also seem conditions that victims and their families in all jurisdictions might reasonably expect to find when involved in such cases, and that the criminal-justice system in all jurisdictions might reasonably take as goals for immediate improvement of their effectiveness.

In addition to these general features of successful community programs, there are some more specific steps that can help reduce the barriers to, and hazards of, prosecution in such cases. These specific steps apply at different stages of the criminal-justice process.

Alternatives to a Court Appearance by the Child

The heart of a child sexual-assault case is the child's testimony, but this need not always be given in court. In some jurisdictions, grand jury indictments can be obtained on the basis of the child's out-of-court deposition, in some cases even using videotaped testimony. In general, grand jury settings are not so formal, nor the rules of evidence so stringent, as a courtroom trial by *petit* jury.

Given an indictment, offenders are more likely to plead guilty—thus sparing the child a courtroom appearance—when there is a range of sentencing alternatives available. Accused offenders who are judged to be amenable to treatment can be offered a recommendation for treatment—along with or instead of incarceration—in exchange for a guilty plea. A number of states operate such treatment facilities within their correctional system (Brecher, 1978). Some of them combine community-based treatment programs for offenders who have been placed on probation with secure facilities for more dangerous offenders. The latter systems seem to work best, both for the offenders and for the justice system (Conte & Berliner, 1983).

Preparing the Child for a Court Appearance

From the beginning of a case, even before it is known whether a trial will take place, the personnel responsible for carrying through the legal procedures must assume that the child may have to testify. If the child eventually does testify, it is likely that the child's word will be pitted against that of the adult defendant. The attorney who may present the child as witness should do everything possible from the outset to give the child emotional support and accurate information about what will ensue. The first step is to establish rapport with the child. This can be facilitated by having the initial interviews in surroundings that are comfortable and nonthreatening for the child. Some time should be spent in getting acquainted. Early on, when the need for a trial is still uncertain, the attorney may want to explore how well the child can talk about what happened. When it becomes clear that a trial is likely and that the child's testimony will be needed, the attorney should try to arrange an opportunity for the child to become familiar with the physical arrangements of a courtroom, and must insure that the child is prepared for the procedural arrangements as well. For example, the child should know, in advance, that the accused will be in the courtroom during the child's testimony, that the defense attorney will cross-examine, and what that cross-examination will be like. The child should be instructed not to answer questions that he or she does not understand, but instead to ask for clarification before answering. The child should be instructed to tell the truth—no matter what—and the attorney should explain to the child how important telling the truth is in the legal process.

The Court Appearance

In most jurisdictions, young children must be qualified as witnesses by the judge before they are permitted to testify before the jury. To qualify a child as a witness, the attorney must demonstrate to the judge's satisfaction that the child (a) can receive and relate information accurately, (b) can understand the difference between telling the truth and telling a lie, and (c) can appreciate the necessity of telling the truth in court. This can be done rather easily even with children as young as 3 or 4 years of age, provided the questions are asked in a way that the child can understand and provided he or she has been prepared to undergo such questioning.

The first test can be met by questioning the child about familiar everyday events: school, playmates, a hobby. Children as young as 3 or 4 can describe familiar events and give accurate information about them (Nelson, 1978). It is also fairly easy to demonstrate the child's knowledge of the difference between a truth and a lie, but not by asking for definitions. Most children, and for that matter most adults, cannot give good definitions of such abstractions. Instead, examples of clear facts and errors of fact should be used ("If I said 'You are wearing a red dress,' would that be a lie or the truth?"). Most children can answer such questions easily and convincingly.

The third test, that of the child's appreciation of the need for truth in the courtroom, is somewhat more abstract. It can sometimes be demonstrated by asking the child about the consequences that usually follow the telling of a lie in everyday life, and then by shifting the topic to the courtroom and getting the child to promise to tell the truth in court.

Not all children can be qualified. Very young children below the age of 3, although they have memories and can communicate in a rudimentary way (Perlmutter, 1980), may simply not be able to meet the legal criteria. Unless there are other witnesses, or physical evidence of the assault, there may be no way to provide evidence of the sexual assault of infants and preverbal children, even though such abuse does take place. Some older children, too, cannot be qualified as witnesses because the postassault psychological effects can include problems of memory and concentration.

After the child has been qualified as a witness, the testimony itself begins. This process is difficult for the child, and can lead to unexpected results. It is important that attorneys remain alert to potential problems, and try to deal with them by using procedures that may be unusual but are not improper or illegal. For example, sometimes a child seems truly terrified at taking the witness stand alone. In such cases, the problem might be solved by having the child sit on the lap of a familiar adult while testifying. Such a procedure may seem foreign to judges and attorneys, but there is no rule in any jurisdiction that forbids it, provided the child's testimony is not prompted. As another example, children are extremely literal in their answers to questions. This can sometimes lead to situations in which adults think the child is being self-contradictory when he or she is simply being concrete. The attorney needs to be alert to such child–

adult misunderstandings, and find ways to restate questions so that the meanings of the child's answers are clear to the adults.

A child's approach to answering questions can have serious consequences for the unwary attorney. In the following case example, a 5-year-old child, on direct examination, told the jury about her father putting his penis in her mouth. On cross-examination by the father's defense attorney, the following exchange took place:

Defense Attorney: And then you said you put your mouth on his penis?

Child: No.

Defense Attorney: You didn't say that?

Child: No.

Defense Attorney: Did you ever put your mouth on his penis?

Child: No.

Defense Attorney: Well, why did you tell your mother that your dad put his penis in your mouth?

Child: My brother told me to.

At this point, it looked as if the child had completely recanted her earlier testimony about the sexual abuse and had only fabricated the story because her brother told her to. However, the experienced prosecuting attorney recognized the problem and clarified the situation:

Prosecuting Attorney: Jennie, you said that you didn't put your mouth on daddy's penis. Is that right?

Child: Yes.

Prosecuting Attorney: Did daddy put his penis in your mouth?

Child: Yes.

Prosecuting Attorney: Did you tell your mom?

Child: Yes.

Prosecuting Attorney: What made you decide to tell?

Child: My brother and I talked about it, and he said I better tell or dad would just keep doing it.

As another example, children sometimes become embarrassed or reluctant to answer questions about the sexual activity. This situation can be helped by using anatomically correct dolls, with the child demonstrating the acts with the dolls while the attorney describes those actions for the written record.

Cross-examination is especially difficult for child witnesses. The defense attorney's job is to impeach the child's testimony. Usual cross-examination tactics, such as bringing up other situations that tend to cast doubt on the witness's veracity or competence or using an intimidating manner in the questioning, are less acceptable in the case of child witnesses and should not go unchallenged. Sometimes judges will intervene to shield child witnesses from such practices. When that does not occur, the prosecuting attorney must do so.

Bolstering the Child's Testimony With Supporting Evidence

However well the child testifies in court, the attorney must always try to support that testimony with as much other evidence as possible. Such corroborating evidence might come from any of several sources: the child's earlier, out-of-court statements; the offender's admissions; medical evidence; and evidence of experts on child sexual abuse.

Some of the most powerful potential evidence in cases of child sexual abuse lies in the child's prior out-of-court statements. When a child first reveals that there has been sexual abuse, the content and manner of the revelation is often striking in its clarity and ring of truth. For example, one 7-year-old girl said casually to her father: "Daddy, does milk come out of your wiener? It comes out of Uncle Bob's and it tastes yukky." There could be little doubt that the child making such a startling statement has been sexually abused. But by the time the child gives testimony in a court, the description of sexual abuse will probably be flat and cursory, and may even appear rehearsed.

There are certain exceptions to the hearsay rule that sometimes permit the child's out-of-court statements to be entered as evidence. One of them is for "excited utterances" (*res gestae*), statements made soon after a traumatic event while the person is still emotionally upset. Unfortunately, this exception is of limited use in child sexual-abuse cases, because children rarely tell of the abuse soon after the event. In some jurisdictions, prosecutors have successfully argued for an expansion of the rule to cover a longer period of time, based on the particular nature of child sexual abuse. Another potential exception to the hearsay rule is for statements made to a medical doctor. Although children are rarely injured when they are molested, medical care may be necessary to rule out infection. If the child tells or shows the doctor where the sexual contact took place, this may be introduced as evidence as part of the medical record.

Another potential source of evidence supporting the child's testimony is from the offender's own admissions. In a surprising proportion of child sexual-abuse cases, the defendant will voluntarily make damaging statements. It is common for accused molesters to tell how the children were the aggressors and they the victims; or to admit touching the child but assert that it was for nonsexual reasons. These statements can sometimes be very useful in supporting the child's testimony. Sometimes they are made to police after Miranda rights have been read; sometimes such admissions are made to friends, relatives, or spouse. While testimony of spouses is not permitted in most kinds of cases, many jurisdictions allow the spouse's testimony if the child of the accused is the victim of the alleged crime. Even statements about the sexual abuse made to psychiatrists or psychologists may be admissible. Normally, information which is disclosed to a therapist cannot be revealed without the consent of the client. Nevertheless, most jurisdictions have laws requiring the reporting of child sexual abuse, thus abrogating the client/therapist privilege in this situation.

Medical evidence can corroborate a child's testimony of sexual abuse, but molestation, though coercive, is seldom so violent as to cause medically specifiable trauma. Medical experts are more likely to contribute to the prosecution by explaining why it is not reasonable to expect identifiable trauma rather than by documenting its presence.

Other experts on child abuse can sometimes contribute by testifying about the dynamics of child sexual abuse. Such expert testimony has been used in some jurisdictions, and has been upheld on appeal in the state of Oregon (*The United States Law Week*, 1983). Such expert testimony most often is used to rebut defense contentions, such as "If this really happened, the child would have told someone right away." Child sexual-abuse experts can provide information about typical child reactions to sexual abuse, including certain symptoms characteristic of posttraumatic stress in such cases: disturbances in physical and cognitive functioning, re-experiencing the traumatic event, withdrawal from usual and familiar activities, and numbing of affective responses (American Psychiatric Association, 1980). While such experts cannot testify to the truthfulness of the child's statements, they can provide the judge and jury a richer context within which to interpret the child's testimony.

When the Child Should Not Testify

From a prosecutor's standpoint, the child victim should testify only when that testimony will substantially increase the chance of a conviction and will not do serious harm to the child. Some cases do not meet those conditions. If the child is unable or unwilling to give a coherent statement and there is no other evidence, the case cannot proceed. Sometimes, even if the child can give a statement, there may be so little chance of conviction that it is not worth putting the child through the stress of the proceedings.

Another issue is the child's own "record." If the child has adjustment problems or a history of trouble, that record will undoubtedly be used to try to impeach him or her in court. It may seem so likely that a jury will be influenced by these background facts that there is little hope for a conviction—hence no purpose in having the child testify. Furthermore, the trauma of being publicly discredited, either by cross-examination or by an acquittal, might be so overwhelming as to exacerbate the child's previous problems.

Yet, it is a mistake for prosecutors to assume, in general, that juries cannot untangle these issues. The probability of winning cannot be the only criterion for filing a charge. And if the more difficult cases are never filed, the opportunity to change the climate within the legal system, and within the society as a whole, will be lost.

Even if charges are filed, the child's behavior on the stand may lead the prosecution, or the parents, to end the proceedings. If the child freezes in the courtroom setting, or is very upset, and if efforts to comfort and support the child fail, it is better to dismiss the case than to proceed. Under these circumstances, no outcome would justify the child's ordeal.

On the other hand, the experience of testifying in court can have a therapeutic effect for the child victim. The child can learn that social institutions take children seriously. Some children report feeling empowered by their participation in the process. Some have complained, when the offender pled guilty, that they did not have an opportunity to be heard in court.

Still, an acquittal can have a devastating effect on the child victim/witness. It is very difficult to explain to children that telling the truth does not always result in an outcome they consider just. The responsible adults must mitigate these effects both by pretrial preparation and by posttrial follow-up. It is essential that the child understand beforehand that court is not a forum for finding out what happened, but rather a very special system by which society tries to identify and control offenders, and that it has a special set of rules for arriving at a result. If there is an acquittal, and even if there is a conviction, children are likely to need follow-up counseling to help resolve their emotional conflicts about the experience—both the abuse and the legal process.

CONCLUDING COMMENTS

We have noted the prevalence of child sexual abuse and de-scribed certain barriers to its successful prosecution. The barriers are not insurmountable. We have noted three general features of success-ful community programs for dealing with child sexual abuse, and a number of specific steps that the responsible adults in such cases (judges, prosecutors, legal-system personnel, medical personnel, par-ents) can take, both to further the successful prosecution of such cases and to minimize further trauma to the child.

The operation of any criminal-justice system requires a careful balancing of the interests of all parties: the child victim/witness, the accused offender, the family, the legal system, and the community. We argue that the current system is out of balance in ways that do not always do full justice to the interests of the child victim/witness. That imbalance needs to be redressed, and we believe it can be done in ways that do not seriously threaten the legitimate interests of the other parties. We have suggested some of those ways throughout this paper, and will recapitulate the most important of them below.

Community programs dealing with child sexual abuse must have appropriately trained professional staff, must have a criminal justice system that can respond flexibly to the special needs of children as victims and as witnesses, and must make use of settings and proce-dures that offer maximum comfort and support for the child who is enmeshed in such legal proceedings. The responsible adults must establish a climate of belief within which the child's competence and credibility is regarded as neither more nor less problematic than that of adults under comparable circumstances. The legal system must adapt its rules of evidence to fit the nature of the crime. For exam-ple, there need to be changes in the statutes of limitation for child sexual abuse, since most children do not report the crime imme-diately after it occurs, and since the first adults to whom they report it often do not believe them and therefore do not act at once on the information. Some states have recently extended their statutes of limitation for such offenses. As another example, there needs to be a broader interpretation of *res gestae* and other exceptions to the hear-say rule to take into account the special circumstances of child sexual abuse (e.g., the likely delay in reporting, the low probability that there were direct witnesses other than the victim, the likelihood that the criminal activities were more clearly described on the first, out-of-court telling than on later, in-court retelling). Such changes have recently been enacted in Washington (State of Washington Law, 1982), permitting statements made outside the court by child victims of sexual abuse to be admitted at the judge's discretion.

Child sexual abuse occurs in part because of the inequalities between child and adult in size, knowledge, and power. The legal system should not perpetuate these same inequalities by failing to take such differences into account. A criminal-justice system fails if it does not protect its most vulnerable and innocent members at least as well as the more powerful.

REFERENCES

American Psychiatric Association, (1980). *Diagnostic and statistical manual of mental disorders* (3rd ed.). Washington, DC: Author.

Brecher, E.M. (1978). *Treatment programs for sexual offenders.* Washington, DC: Department of Justice.

Bulkley, J. (1981a). *Child sexual abuse and the law.* Washington, DC: American Bar Association.

Bulkley, J. (1981b). *Innovations in prosecution of child sexual abuse cases.* Washington, DC: American Bar Association.

Burgess, A., Groth, A.N. Holmstrom, L.L., & Sgroi, S. (1978). *Sexual assault of children and adolescents.* Lexington, MA: D.C. Heath.

Conte, J., & Berliner, L. (1981). Sexual abuse of children: Implications for practice. *Social Casework, 62*(10), 601–606.

Conte, J., & Berliner, L. (1983). Prosecution of the offender in cases of sexual assault against children. *Victimology, 8,* 102–109.

Finkelhor, D. (1979). *Sexual victimization of children.* New York: Free Press.

Gentry, C. (1978). Incestuous abuse of children: The need for an objective view. *Child Welfare, 57*(6), 356.

Groth, A.N., & Birnbaum, H. (1979). *Men who rape: The psychology of the offender.* New York: Plenum.

Herman, J. (1981). *Father-daughter incest.* Cambridge, MA: Harvard University Press.

Johnson, M.K., & Foley, M.A. (1984). Differentiating fact from fantasy: The reliability of children's memory. *Journal of Social Issues. 40*(2), 33–50.

Kroth, J. (1979). *Child sexual abuse: Analysis of a family therapy approach.* Springfield, IL: Charles C. Thomas.

Marin, B.V., Holmes, D.L., Guth, M., & Kovac, P. (1979). The potential of children as eyewitnesses. *Law and Human Behavior. 3,* 295–306.

Masson, J.M. (1984). *The assault on truth: Freud's suppression of the seduction theory.* New York: Farrar, Straus, & Giraux.

Nelson, K. (1978). How young children represent knowledge of their world in and out of language. In R. Siegler (Ed.), *Children's thinking: What develops?* (pp. 255–273). Hillside, NJ: Erlbaum.

Perlmutter, M. (Ed.), (1980). *Children's memory.* San Francisco. California: Jossey-Bass.

Rush, F. (1977). The Freudian coverup. *Chrysalis. 1,* 31–45.

Russell, D. (1982). The incidence and prevalence of intrafamilial and extrafamilial sexual abuse of female children. *Child Abuse and Neglect: The International Journal.* (Special Issue of Child Sexual Abuse). *7,* 133–146.

Sarafino, E.P. (1979). An estimate of nationwide incidence of sexual offenses against children. *Child Welfare. 58,* 127–132.

The United States Law Week. 2-22-83. 51 LW 2484, 1983.

State of Washington. Laws of 1982, Chapter 29.

When Systems Fail: Protecting the Victim of Child Sexual Abuse

by Vincent J. Fontana

Child fatalities, retardation syndromes and psychological damage resulting from child maltreatment provide glaring evidence that systems have failed these innocent victims. Children are being victimized by our human frailties, and by our lack of commitment and concern.

What is the "system"? As used here, the system consists of a conglomerate of people with various responsibilities and expertise. When we speak of a child protective system in a community, we think of a child protective agency, or an office of Special Services for Children, or the Society for the Prevention of Cruelty to Children. In reality, the child protective system of any community encompasses the board of education, the police department, the district attorney, the medical establishment, voluntary private child care agencies, the foster care system, the family court and last, but not least, the child protective agency. The entire system is manned by people—some more caring, trained and dedicated than others. Failures in the system result as a natural consequence of large caseloads, too much paper work, faulty supervision and poor judgement.

If the inadequacies and failures of the system are to be analyzed and documented, the entire child protective system must be appraised. To criticize and find remedies for one part of the system while ignoring the others is an unfulfilling exercise in futility, besides being a waste of money and effort.

Vincent J. Fontana is Medical Director of the New York Foundling Hospital, Center for Parent and Child Development, New York, NY. "When Systems Fail: Protecting the Victim of Child Sexual Abuse" is reprinted from *Children Today,* July/August 1984, volume 13, number 4, pp. 14–18. Reprinted by permission of the author.

The daily frustrations encountered in dealing with the protection of young children clearly indicate that blame should be placed on all parts of the system. The lack of coordination, communication and cooperation between and among responsible agencies is the source of the trouble.

In the area of child sexual abuse, the failures in the system are insidious but nonetheless damaging. Unfortunately, these failures are not due to lack of knowledge but to failure to act and to make basic changes based on what is known.

Disagreement over the definition of child sexual abuse, problems involved in observing and documenting private events and the stigma associated with sexual abuse impede efforts to intervene and effectively assist. In addition, sexual abuse is substantially different from physical abuse of children in etiology, occurrence and reporting. There is a lack of clarity regarding what is reportable as suspected sexual abuse. Laws speak of "reasonable cause"—a standard legal phrase implying a lower threshold of information on which to act than the "probable cause" standard governing police intervention in suspected crime.

Professionals in the fields of medicine, education and social work require operational definitions of "reasonable cause" for suspected child abuse situations. Working out clearly defined criteria for reporting sexual abuse will assist in the prevention of some of the failures attributed to the system. Although there is a tendency to equate intrafamilial child sexual abuse and the sexual victimization of children by strangers, the two are very different and require very different intervention approaches. In intrafamilial cases, which is the focus here, the relationship between the child and the offending adult exists in a far wider and deeper context than the victimization act itself, and violence or threats of violence are rare. This adds enormously to the complexity of the situation, and it means that the event and the intervention are likely to have a greater impact on the child and family.

By definition, an obvious and important goal of intervention is amelioration of the consequences of intrafamilial child sexual abuse and the future protection of its victims. Achieving this goal depends upon the ability to alter the personal or environmental factors that were the cause of the abuse. Unfortunately, there is no consensus on treatment goals or treatment approaches. There is considerable disagreement about the basic issue of punishment or treatment of the abuser, with a growing emphasis on a combination of both approaches in a modified form. The long-term effect of these approaches upon the child is unclear and unknown.

Many clinicians and researchers assert that punishment through the criminal justice system is ineffective. They note that an offender may be returned home untreated and that the emphasis on proving the case in criminal court overlooks the child's needs and subjects him or her to the dictates of prosecutory advocacy. Even worse, criminal prosecution subjects an older child to greater stress and tends to make the child feel personally responsible for the parent's imprisonment.

Although some report that criminal prosecution creates resistance in the family as family members rally to the father's defense, others state that prosecution encourages the offender to seek change, thus strengthening his commitment to treatment. Giarretto advocates the use of the criminal justice system in a controlled way that avoids destruction of the family and does not lead to imprisonment.[1] In this approach, the parent is encouraged to turn himself or herself over voluntarily to law enforcement officials and to submit to criminal jurisdiction with the knowledge that imprisonment usually will be avoided through cooperation and adherence to the treatment regimen. To accomplish this purpose, other researchers advocate the use of a family, juvenile or other civil court.

Related to issues surrounding the use of the criminal justice system are the strong feelings usually expressed by social work and medical professionals that the criminal justice system is not sensitive to the needs of the child. Schultz points out that most police and prosecutors have no training in non-damaging ways to interview children, lack understanding of the child's psychosexual stage of development and tend to use adversary approaches appropriate for adults.[2] Sgroi notes that "this is, unfortunately, equally true of child protective service agencies—the workers who investigate sexual abuse cases usually lack the specialized skills, experience, and supervision required to deal with the delicate, volatile, and highly demanding child protective problem yet to be identified."[3] Similarly, Brandt notes that the trauma experienced by children and families can be exacerbated in hospitals or clinics.[4] This issue of interrogation is critical because of its impact on the child victim; interventions which add to the victimization of the child have no true protective value or function.

The need for sensitive handling of the child applies to all systems, but its importance has not yet reached everyone who is likely to respond to a child victim of intrafamilial sexual abuse. While this issue has been raised by the handful of professionals who specialize in the treatment of sexual abuse or incest, such specialists are likely to be among the last to see the child, often some time after identification or discovery of the incident and the initiation of legal intervention. Many more must be reached with information on normal psychosexual child development and correct, age-appropriate ways to talk to a child who may be a victim of sexual abuse.

While there is probably general agreement on the techniques to use, a major difficulty is the uncertainty or disbelief that many feel when a child reports being sexually abused, either directly or indirectly. This is understandable, but it must be overcome. If a child reports being sexually abused, the person in whom the child confides should make a report and give the protective service professionals a chance to assess the child's statements. Under the requirements of state reporting laws, such a statement is sufficient to make a report—to give one reasonable cause to suspect that abuse occurred. A child's statement about being sexually abused is almost universally true; children generally do not lie, fantasize or hallucinate about being sexually abused.

Moreover, there is a simple test that can be applied in many cases, especially with children below the age of puberty. Very young victims of sexual abuse tend to possess a level of detailed knowledge about sexual practices beyond the norm for their age; their sexual awareness is "age inappropriate," a sign that someone has initiated them. Sexually provocative mannerisms in young children are usually an example of age inappropriate behavior. Young children who report sexual abuse should not be dismissed when they act sexually provocative. We have begun to be aware of the bias such behavior frequently creates when adults report being raped. It is even more impermissible in cases involving children. It is important that this point of view be accepted by those who are in a position to deal with children who may be the victims of sexual abuse.

Sensitive handling of the child includes any medical examination that may be performed in an attempt to document and diagnose the possibility of sexual abuse. I am confident that the professionalism of physicians and other medical workers, if supported by adequate training, will assure that the examination does not in itself become another trauma for the child victim. We cannot assume, however, that such training has been provided, and steps must be taken to make sure that it is given as part of medical training in school, in residency and in continuing educational settings.

The literature on the effects of intrafamilial child sexual abuse indicates a strong need for mental health services. Indeed, most of the effects reported are psychological or emotional, with behavioral rather than physical consequences. There seems to be little possibility of long-range physical consequences, but a great possibility of long-range emotional and behavioral damage. There is no debate on whether mental health services are needed—the debate is limited to the type, such as individual, group, conjoint or family therapy, and the correct sequence.

Family therapy has been recommended as the treatment of choice. However, some objections raised to using this approach as the primary one include parental refusal to cooperate, the impact of raising some issues—such as sexual problems between the parents—in front of the child, and the traditional stance of family therapists that all are equally responsible for the situation under treatment. Individual therapy is strongly supported by a number of clinicians, sometimes in conjunction with other types, because it gives a child the greatest chance to ventilate those feelings which might later engender the most trouble.

The difficulties of providing mental health services to victims of intrafamilial child sexual abuse, however, are no different from those encountered in obtaining such services for child protective cases in general. A study conducted for the National Institute of Mental Health pointed out that "mental health professionals are accustomed to working with individuals who are 'motivated' and who actively seek help"; they generally do not have outreach strategies for highly resistant families, and their scheduling practices cannot handle families who frequently miss appointments or come late.[5] Another study of mental health services for abused children found that improvements were dependent upon two conditions: parents who were willing to allow the child to change and to change themselves, and a therapist who was able to influence the environment, such as the school setting and relationships with others, and help the child within the playroom.[6]

Such obstacles to treatment must be understood and corrected if the mental health system is to help child victims of abuse. The likelihood that such treatment will be long-term may conflict with the current emphasis on "cost-effective"—that is, cheap—short-term approaches.

Another issue that impacts heavily on the child is whether he or she is removed from the home as a result of the interventions that follow disclosure of the abuse. Clinicians and researchers disagree on whether or not the child or the adult offender should be removed from the home during treatment, or for longer thereafter. Some advocate separation of the offending parent from the child, usually forcing the parent to live elsewhere during initial treatment. Although, as Coleman notes, the police usually remove the child to preserve evidence and to prevent the child from being pressured to change his or her story,[7] a number of researchers recommend against removing the child unless there is some compelling reason because it may be difficult to reunite the child and the family later. Zaphiris, who believes that removal of the child may contribute to his or her victimization by exacerbating feelings of blame for the incest, recommends removal only if the incest is a symptom of other serious pathology, which he believes is seldom the case, or if it is concurrent with physical abuse.[8] Still others believe that removal of the child is ineffective under any circumstances, hence of no purpose.

The debate over the best or most appropriate intervention into intrafamilial child sexual abuse cases makes at least one thing clear: the chance that the intervention, and the system offering it, may fail, or even harm, the child victim is greater than we wish to acknowledge.

The literature offers conflicting advice on the relative merits of the social service and criminal justice approaches to intrafamilial child sexual abuse, and it offers equally conflicting advice on the most appropriate or necessary immediate intervention. While the best answer might be that such decisions should depend upon the specifics of each case, policy decisions in many states are increasing the involvement of the criminal justice approach.

A recent California case, for example, has received widespread attention. Media accounts gave the impression that a child was sent to jail for refusing to testify against her stepfather, who was reported for sexual abuse after voluntarily seeking therapy. California is one state that uses the criminal justice system to "encourage" an offending adult to seek treatment. However, the fact that it was necessary to "encourage" the stepfather *after* he sought treatment indicates that the intent of the California system was not carried through. But the case has wider implications in all states that are promoting greater use of the criminal justice system to gain leverage over offending adults.

The California child was "sent to jail" because the criminal justice system followed one of its usual procedures for dealing with recalcitrant material witnesses, who are usually incarcerated to "encourage" them to be more cooperative. Unfortunately, in this case the witness was a child and the victim of the "criminal complaint." Clearly, what is an appropriate method of dealing with an adult became a savagely inappropriate method of responding to a terrified child.

Law enforcement officials have an obligation to define and create safeguards to protect children from techniques which have been developed to deal with adults but which result in serious damage when applied to a child. This will not be an easy task because it confronts established methods that reflect standard practices which have evolved from dealing with adult defendants and witnesses in criminal trials.

Methods must be found to protect child victims from further emotional abuse. Testimony videotaped for later replay or taken in the judge's chambers with key participants present are techniques well worth exploring.

A long delay between steps in the judicial process seriously limits a child's ability to testify and inflicts further hurt to the child. Children have difficulty remembering. With the passage of time, details become indistinct. Investigations must be handled with speed and without interruption in an effort to minimize the effects of the failures of our difficult and complicated legal system. With a speedy, coordinated investigatory and prosecutory effort, further psychological trauma to the child and family will be decreased.

In formulating a set of guidelines for investigating child sexual abuse, two distinct lines of approach must be considered: law enforcement and child protective services. In law enforcement, the purpose of the investigation is to obtain evidence for criminal prosecution; in child protective services, the purpose is to assess the risk to the child in order to take protective action and offer treatment. There is an urgent need for cooperation between law enforcement and child protective agencies to integrate their approach toward both the child victim and the adult offender.

The attention given to child sexual abuse is recent. It is, perhaps, the last type of child abuse to be recognized for the serious problem it is. This attention comes at a time of dwindling resources for treatment services—an experience unlike the growth in services which paralleled the increased attention to child abuse and neglect in the 1970s. This is unfortunate, because it increases the likelihood that the new attention will not result in increased resources for treatment. In fact, it may serve to further impede efforts as resources for dealing with child abuse and neglect in general are stretched to respond to increased reports of child sexual abuse.

Nationally, the protective service caseload is burgeoning, and evidence is accumulating that resources for staff and services have not kept pace, causing child protective services in this country to be functioning at less than acceptable levels. Yet we must continue efforts to improve the protection of all neglected and abused children, regardless of the problems we adults encounter in providing and securing the help they need. Limitations of fiscal resources or lack of knowledge must not become another source of victimization for the children in need of our protection.

These matters are far from cut and dried—they are real problems and issues; they are the reasons why systems fail. They must be systematically studied in order to develop standardized medical, legal and social procedures for dealing with child sexual abuse. A unified effort at networking by these involved groups is urgent if we are to prevent further hurt to child victims.

REFERENCES

1. H. Giarretto, "Humanistic Treatment of Father-Daughter Incest," in R.R. Helfer and C.H. Kempe (Eds.), *Child Abuse and Neglect: The Family and the Community,* Cambridge, Ballinger, 1976.

2. L.G. Schultz, "The Child Victim: Social, Psychological, and Legal Perspectives," *Child Welfare,* Mar. 1973.

3. S.M. Sgroi, "Introduction: A National Needs Assessment for Protecting Child Victims of Sexual Assault," in A.W. Burgess, A.N. Groth, L.L. Holmstrom and S.M. Sgroi (Eds.), *Sexual Assault of Children and Adolescents,* Lexington, Mass., Lexington Books, 1978.

4. R.S.T. Brandt, "Manual on Sexual Abuse and Misuse of Children," Boston, Mass., Judge Baker Guidance Center, undated.

5. M.B. Holmes, et al., *Child Abuse and Neglect Programs: Practice and Theory,* National Institute of Mental Health, U.S. Dept. of Health, Education and Welfare, Pub. No. (ADM) 77–344, Washington, D.C., 1977.

6. P. Beezley, et al., "Psychotherapy," in H. Martin (Ed.), *The Abused Child: A Multi-Disciplinary Approach to Developmental Issues and Treatment,* Cambridge, Ballinger Publishing Co., 1976.

7. P.F. Coleman, "Incest: Family Treatment Model," Pierce County Child Protective Services, Washington State Department of Social Services, undated.

8. A.G. Zaphiris, "Incest: The Family with Two Known Victims," Denver, American Humane Association, undated.

SECTION V

The Abuser

Introduction

The child molester, or pedophile, is probably, as far as the general public is concerned, the lowest of criminals. The nature of the deed negates any sympathy, and when imprisoned, the molester is often in actual physical danger. Even in the social strata of criminals, the child molester is at the bottom.

Yet a handful of professionals have been able to sort through this emotional morass and catch a glimpse of the abuser's basic humanity. In direct response to that humanity, they have begun to work in sustained efforts to change or inhibit the molester's sexual preferences. It is the work of these psychiatrists, social workers, and psychologists that this closing section discusses.

In their article, "The Child Molester: Clinical Observations," Dr. Nicholas Groth, William Hobson, and Thomas Gary provide an overall view of the abuser garnered from their many years experience in the field. Here, they dispell myths, define terms, discuss observations, and offer suggestions for treatment.

Dr. Fred Berlin and Edgar Krout survey the diagnosis and treatment of pedophiles in "Pedophilia: Diagnostic Concepts Treatment, and Ethical Considerations." In their closing paragraphs, ethical considerations are posed that offer a worthy conclusion to this study of the pedophile.

The Child Molester: Clinical Observations

by A. Nicholas Groth, William F. Hobson, and Thomas S. Gary

INTRODUCTION

An increasing amount of attention is being focused on the sexual
victimization of children, yet no exact statistics exist in regard to this
problem for a number of reasons: Many such victimizations may go
unreported or undetected, or the suspect may not be apprehended; or
there may be insufficient evidence to go to court; or the offender is
not convicted; or even if he is convicted his offense may fall under a
number of different statutes which are not age-specific—in Massachusetts, for example, the sexual victimization of a child can be encompassed under 25 different statutes—and therefore it is impossible to
retrieve the number of identified sexual offenses committed specifically against children. Nevertheless human service and criminal justice professionals are encountering more and more reported incidents
of inter-generation sexual activity. The authors of this chapter are
clinicians who have worked with identified sexual offenders against
children in a variety of institutional and community-based settings.
Our professional experience to date has spanned 16 years and encompassed over 500 such offenders, and our aim in this chapter is to
share our clinical observations, ideas, and impressions derived from
our work in the hope that this will offer others a useful overview and
approach to understanding and working with the child molester. Our

A. Nicholas Groth is Director of the Sex Offender Program in Somers,
Connecticut and is co-author of *Men Who Rape: The Psychology of the
Offender*. William F. Hobson is a clinical psychologist and Co-director of the
program at Somers, Connecticut. They are co-authors of "The Child Molester:
Clinical Observations" with Thomas S. Gary. This article was reprinted from
Social Work and Child Sexual Abusers by Jon R. Conte and David A. Shore,
eds., pp. 129–144. Copyright © 1982 by the Haworth Press, 28 East 22nd
Street, New York, NY. Reprinted by permission of the publisher.

sample of identified offenders may be biased—there may be better integrated individuals who commit similar offenses with more discretion and circumspection and thus remain undetected—but our offenders have in fact encompassed a sufficiently broad spectrum in regard to age, education, and occupation to persuade us that the fact of identification and conviction is not a distorting variable with regard to the psychology of the child offender. With increasing opportunity to work with and study such offenders our knowledge of the offender, his offense, and his victim continues to develop, and we find that many of the commonly held assumptions in regard to the child molester (pedophile) are not being substantiated.

MYTHS ABOUT CHILD MOLESTATION

Generally in order to safeguard children against sexual victimization, they are admonished to watch out for advances from strangers. For the most part, however, the child molester is not a stranger, the large majority being in fact known and often related to their victims. The child molester is commonly stereotyped as a "dirty old man" or a "monster." The fact is that in more than half the cases we have worked with we found that the offender had attempted or committed his first sexual assault by the age of 16. Although most identified offenders are adults this only reflects the point at which their behavior is recognized as an offense, not the onset of their sexual pathology. Because the sexual victimization of children is so reprehensible, the offender is perceived to be some sort of depraved monster. Again in our experience we have by and large not found this to be the case. His offense has been more the product of immaturity than malicious intent, and in many respects the offender may otherwise be living a competent, law-abiding, and productive life. Unfortunately, when people expect the offender to be a monster and the accused is a respectable person, then doubt is shed on the veracity of the victim's allegations—the child is thought to be mistaken of even lying. Generally speaking we have not found any social or demographic characteristics that differentiate the child molester from the general population, not his race, religion, intelligence, education, vocation, socioeconomic class, or the like. What we have found is that pedophilia cuts across the whole spectrum of diagnostic categories, but for the most part we are not dealing with persons who are mentally ill but who are emotionally troubled. The defects in their functioning are not cognitive, or perceptual, or emotional, but interpersonal. What we are dealing with, in most cases, is the aftermath of physical and/or psychological abuse, neglect, exploitation, and/or abandonment during the offender's formative years which has precluded the development of a sense of relatedness to others.

We have also observed that alcohol and drug abuse play a relatively minor role in the commission of such offenses, that females as well as males sexually molest children although such offenses are less socially visible and under-reported, that preadolescent boys and girls are at equal risk of being sexually victimized, and that men who sexually molest boys are misidentified as homosexuals when they are in fact pedophiles. Finally the child molester is the recipient of the strongest societal anger and disapproval which ironically only confirms his perception of adults as hostile and punitive and reinforces his attraction to children. If we are genuinely concerned about combatting the sexual victimization of children we must be humanistic in our attitudes towards the offender so that we don't inadvertantly perpetuate the problem. If part of the reason the offender turns to children is because he is intimidated by adults and he is then placed in a prison setting which exposes him to threats of harm, humiliation, exploitation, and physical abuse at the hands of other inmates, this may serve only to reinforce his fear, distrust, and avoidance of adults and to encourage his seeking out children whom he perceives will not hate or hurt him. Where incarceration is required, then, a security treatment center specifically for sex offenders is preferable to a conventional correctional institution or prison.

THE OFFENSE

What is child sexual victimization? It is any behavior on the part of an individual that exposes a child to the risk of psychological interference in his or her sexual development. The spectrum of such victimization may range from situations at one extreme in which there is no direct physical contact with the victim (for example, the offender may expose himself or he may encourage children to permit him to photograph them in the nude) to those at the other extreme in which the child may be physically attacked and injured or even killed. Sexual offenses against children can be classified into two basic categories in regard to the mode of aggression exhibited in the offense: child molesters and child rapists. Some offenders gain sexual access to the child through a combination of enticement and deception. They lure or trick the child into the sexual activity; reward the child for his or her participation; and caution the child against disclosure. These non-violent offenders, whom we refer to as *child molesters*, essentially coax or pressure the child into the sexual activity. Their offenses constitute sexual extortion in which the child is taught to provide sex in exchange for attention, acceptance, recognition, and material gain. Other offenders resort to threat, intimidation, and physical force to achieve submission on the part of the victim. They are *child rapists* who overpower and/or threaten to harm their victims. Their offenses constitute sexual attacks in which the child victim relinquishes sex in return for survival and release. Obviously the child rapist poses a more serious risk to the physical safety of the victim than does the child molester, but fortunately child rapists constitute a small minority of the sexual offenders against children. For this reason the remainder of this chapter will focus on the major type of perpetrator of sexual offenses against children: the child molester.

Definition

What is a child molester? As it is used in this chapter, the term "child-molester" refers to a significantly older person whose conscious sexual interests and overt sexual behaviors are directed either partially or exclusively towards prepubertal children. In contrast to the child rapist for whom sexual aggression is a hostile act, the child-molester exhibits a positive emotional investment in the child which he eroticizes. He seeks to establish an on-going relationship with the child w' .ch includes but extends beyond sexual activity. Having first establis ied a non-sexual relationship and position of familiarity with the child he gradually indoctrinates the child into sexual activities which ecome more advanced over time. He behaves in counter-aggressive ways, however, and should the child refuse or resist his sexual advances, the child molester may increase his efforts at enticement and manipulation but will not resort to physical force. If the child actively and persistently resists the child-molester will ultimately turn to another, more accommodating victim. The risk to the victim of the child-molester, then, is not one of physical injury, but one of psychological harm.

Typology

One of the most basic observations that can be made about child offenders is that they are not all alike, and our aim in this chapter is to differentiate among various patterns of pedophilic behavior and to identify different types of child molesters. Sexual offenders against children can be divided into two basic types on the basis of their level of socio-sexual maturation: (1) the *fixated* offender whose primary sexual orientation is towards children, and (2) the *regressed* offender whose sexual involvement with a child is a clear departure, under stress, from a primary sexual orientation towards agemates. (See Table 1.)

Table 1: Typology of Child Molesters

FIXATED TYPE

1. Primary sexual orientation is to children.
2. Pedophilic interests begin at adolescence.
3. No precipitating stress/no subjective distress.
4. Persistent interest and compulsive behavior.
5. Premeditated, pre-planned offenses.
6. IDENTIFICATION: offender identifies closely with the victim and equalizes his behavior to the level of the child and/or may adopt a pseudo-parental role to the victim.
7. Male victims are primary targets.
8. Little or no sexual contact initiated with agemates; offender is usually single or in a marriage of convenience.
9. Usually no history of alcohol or drug abuse and offense is not alcohol related.
10. Characterological immaturity; poor sociosexual peer relationships.
11. Offense = maladaptive resolution of life development (maturation) issues.

REGRESSED TYPE

1. Primary sexual orientation is to agemates.
2. Pedophilic interests emerge in adulthood.
3. Precipitating stress usually evident.
4. Involvements may be more episodic and may wax and wane with stress.
5. Initial offense may be impulsive and not premeditated.
6. SUBSTITUTION: offender replaces conflictual adult relationship with involvement with a child; victim is a pseudoadult substitute and in incest situations the offender abandons his parental role.
7. Female victims are primary targets.
8. Sexual contact with a child coexists with sexual contact with agemates; offender is usually married or common-law.
9. Offense is often alcohol related.
10. More traditional lifestyle but under-developed peer relationships.
11. Offense = maladaptive attempt to cope with specific life stresses.

FIXATED CHILD MOLESTER

For one type of offender his sexual attraction to children constitutes an arrestment of his sociosexual maturation resulting from unresolved formative issues which undermined his subsequent development and persist in his personality functioning. Such an offender exhibits a compulsive attraction to and sexual fixation on children. From the onset of his adolescence children have been the primary or exclusive object of his sexual interests and any sexual contact with age mates that occurs is usually situational in nature, initiated by the other individual involved, and never replaces his preference for and chronic sexual involvement with children.

Clinical Example of a Fixated Offender

Scott is a 20 year old, white, single male of average intelligence who is the product of alcoholic parents and an abusive home. He became aware of his sexual attraction to preadolescent boys when he himself was 13 years old. Scott would sexually approach neighborhood children and engage them in mutual fondling, masturbation, and fellatio: "I would run around making every kid in sight—anyone younger than I was. I'd talk them into it. I'd masturbate just looking at a boy, or fondle him, play with his ass, kiss him, and blow him. I enjoyed being with younger kids." When he was 17 Scott left home and earned a living as a male prostitute and model for pornographic films. In this activity he would engage in sexual relations with adult males and on a few occasions with adult females, but although he would perform sexually with adults and agemates for money, he never experienced being sexually attracted to men or women and found himself "turned-on" only to boys between the ages of 10 and 12.

REGRESSED CHILD MOLESTER

For another type of offender his sexual involvement with a child constitutes a temporary or permanent departure from his more characteristic attraction to age mates. Such a regressed offender did not previously exhibit any predominant sexual interest in significantly younger persons (during his formative years) but when he entered adulthood and experienced the attendant responsibilities and life-demands as overwhelming and/or when his adult relationships became conflictual and emotionally unfulfilling, a sexual attraction to children emerged. Such cross-generational sexual activity is typically activated by some precipitating stress and may wax and wane in response to the amount of stress the offender experiences in coping with adult life demands.

Clinical Example of a Regressed Offender

Brad is a 37 year old, white, married male of average intelligence. He reports a fairly unremarkable life history. He had no difficulty in school and feels he grew up in a basically stable home. His sexual development does not appear unconventional. As a child he engaged in sexual play and experimentation with his siblings. He began masturbating at age 15 and experienced intercourse at age 19 with a girlfriend he ultimately married. He reports no extra-marital affairs, but became sexually involved with his 11 year old daughter when he lost his job and discovered that his wife had a terminal illness. Under the pressure of mounting medical bills and other responsibilities Brad began drinking heavily. He states "I loved my wife and children and still and always will. I don't know how this happened. There were times I would get into a deep depression and one day I came home and my daughter was asleep on my bed. That's how it began. At first I just touched her but later I started having intercourse with her." Brad's sexual activity continued for two years during which time he did not engage in sexual activities with persons his own age.

DYNAMICS

Cross-generational sexual behavior, then, may constitute a fixation on the part of the offender: a sexual orientation towards children as the result of arrested socio-sexual development; or it may constitute a regression, the result of a sudden or progressive deterioration of emotionally meaningful or gratifying adult relationships. In general, fixated child molesters are drawn to children sexually in that they identify with the child and appear in some ways to want to remain children themselves. It is for this reason that the trend for fixated offenders is to target boys as victims. This does not represent a homosexual object-choice, psychologically, but a narcissistic one. They see the boy as a projected representation of themselves. They feel themselves to be more child than adult—more boys than men—and therefore find themselves more comfortable (especially sexually) in the company of children (boys/girls) than adults (men/women).

Regressed child molesters turn to a child sexually as a substitute for their adult relationships which have become conflictual and emotionally unfulfilling. Since most such offenders are primarily emotionally invested in women in their adult relationships, it is for this reason that the trend for regressed child molesters is to target girls as victims. They select a child (girl), with whom they will feel more competent, to replace the adult (woman) with whom they feel inadequate.

The psychological basis of pedophilia, then, is feelings of inadequacy, immaturity, vulnerability, helplessness, and isolation. Adult sexuality is threatening and, consequently, is avoided or abandonded. The child molester instead relates to a child as if the child were a peer or equal. The fixated offender does this by adapting his interests and behavior to the level of the child, whereas the regressed offender relates to the child as if she or he were an adult. Psychologically the fixated offender experiences himself as a child, whereas the regressed offender experiences the child as a pseudo-adult. For both the victim represents a fantasy. The level of the offender's socio-sexual maturation can be gauged from the age of the victim he characteristically selects.

MOTIVATIONS

What prompts an adult to become sexually involved with a child? Pedophilia is complex and multi-determined. Sexual involvement with a child is by definition coercive on the part of the adult, since the child does not occupy equal power status to the adult. By virtue of being an adult the grownup possesses social authority, physical superiority, wider experience, and greater knowledge than the child. In sexual encounters with adults children may cooperate but they are not capable of giving informed consent. For this reason pedophilia constitutes the sexual abuse of power. As with other forms of sexual assault (rape, indecent exposure, obscene telephone calling, and the like), sexual desire or passion does not appear to be the primary determinant of such behavior. Child molestation is the sexual expression of non-sexual needs and unresolved life issues. Pedophilia goes beyond sexual need and is, ultimately, a pseudo-sexual act.

Through sexual involvement with a child the offender attempts to fulfill his psychological needs for recognition, acceptance, validation, affiliation, mastery, and control. It is not sexual gratification or release, per se, that is the source of the satisfaction the offender finds in his sexual contact with the victim; it is his interpretation of the sexual activity as evidence of the child's acceptance and caring about him. "She was glad to see me;" "He looked up to me;" "She loved me;" "He made me feel important;" are typical comments made by the offender in regard to his victim. In addition he feels more in control in a relationship to a child where there is less risk of an emotionally devastating rebuff or rejection. Nor is his sense of competency threatened by a child who is more accepting and less demanding than an adult.

Intimidated by adult sexuality, the child-molester withdraws to pre-sexual or non-sexual children, typically describing the appeal of children as their being innocent, loving, open, warm, trusting, and clean. Sex is "dirty" and pre-adolescent children are sexless—that is, they do not confront the offender with physical characteristics of adult sexuality: the boy's genitals are small, he does not ejaculate, his body is smooth and hairless; the girl likewise has no pubic hair or breast development, she does not menstruate, she cannot become pregnant. It may seem to be a paradox that the child molester is sexually attracted to a non-sexual person, but it is not a paradox when it is realized that the primary motivation underlying such offenses is not sexual.

It is through the sexual activity with a child that the offender attempts to solve unresolved issues of his development and fulfill unmet needs in his life. It is for this reason that the child molester typically seeks on-going sexual involvement with his victim. He is searching through sex for something that goes beyond sex. Since such sexual behavior cannot ultimately resolve the underlying issues nor meet the unfulfilled needs, it becomes repetitive or compulsive in nature—both self-perpetuating and self-defeating at the same time—and in this respect is equivalent to symptom-formation. Just as an alcoholic is not driven to drink out of thirst, a pedophile is not molesting children simply out of sexual desire.

Generally speaking, the clinical impression that emerges in regard to a child molester is that of an immature individual whose pedophilic behavior serves to compensate for his relative helplessness in meeting adult bio-psycho-social life demands. It offers him a retreat from conflictual adult relationships. It provides a sense of power, control, and competence. It fulfills a longing for intimacy, affection, and affiliation. It validates his worth. And it may provide some sexual gratification. However, all of this is basically illusionary and transient. The child will eventually mature and the offender must then find another victim.

SYMPTOM CHOICE

Why does an individual become sexually drawn to children? Why is pedophilia the symptom that emerges in response to psychological stress? Again, such complex behavior cannot be reduced to a single cause. It may be the product of a number of incompletely understood bio-psycho-social variables, yet the role of sexual victimization in the developmental histories of child molesters appears to be a significant factor. The majority of child molesters that we have worked with have themselves been sexually abused children, and just as the battered child runs a high risk of becoming a battering parent, so too, it appears, does the sexually victimized child—especially the male—run a high risk of becoming a sexual victimizer. Pedophilia, then, may reflect yet another dynamic: an attempt to resolve an unresolved sexual trauma. One way in which the male child may try to combat the feelings of powerlessness inherent in being a victim is to ultimately identify with the aggressor and reverse roles; that is, to become the powerful victimizer rather than the helpless victim. The child molester then re-enacts in his offense the characteristics of his own victimization in an attempt to restore to himself a feeling of being in control. To combat the negative feelings associated with his own victimization he attempts to "romanticize" his sexual offense and regard it as an expression of his caring for the child victim rather than his using the child to meet his own needs (a fact suggested by his emotional over-investment in the child).

It appears to be an inescapable conclusion that pedophilia is one of the possible consequences of child sexual abuse and neglect. For this reason, when working with offenders, it is important to carefully explore what was occurring in their lives especially at the time they were the same age as the child they are victimizing.

TREATMENT

Treatment may be defined as any type of intervention designed to reduce, prevent, or eliminate the risk of the child molester again committing an offense. To achieve this requires effecting changes in the internal psychological predisposition of the offender; in his external living environment; or in both. Essentially, the goal is one of control: either the offender must develop (internal) control over his pedophilic behavior or he must be (externally) controlled so as to prevent his acting out such interests. There are four basic treatment modalities aimed at developing controls over pedophilic urges:

1. *Chemotherapy.* Various antiandrogenic hormones, such as Depo-Provera, have been shown to have a moderating effect on sexual aggressiveness and enhance self-regulation of sexual behavior. Although the use of Depo-Provera in the treatment of sexual offenders is still in the experimental stages, it does offer promise as a chemical control of antisocial sexual behaviors such as pedophilia.

2. *Behavior Modification.* Another approach in working with child offenders is to address the specific behaviors associated with the offense and, through a series of conditioning exercises based on learning principles, to diminish sexual arousal to children and enhance sexual responsiveness to adults. Progress is monitored by physiological measurements of erection responses to relevant stimuli. This modality attempts to change the clients' sexual preferences by making aversive those sexual behaviors which are outlawed and by

replacing them with more socially acceptable sexual behaviors.

3. *Psychotherapy.* This modality encompasses a wide range of approaches based on interpersonal interaction and views the offending sexual behavior as symptomatic of internal emotional conflicts which can be resolved through achieving awareness and better understanding of the underlying issues. Through such introspection the offender is expected to arrive at better controls over his sexually inappropriate behavior.

4. *Psychosocial education.* This modality, which we employ at our facility, views sexual offenses to be the products of defects in human development and attempts to remedy such defects through a combination of re-education, resocialization, and counseling. The aim is to alert the offender to the life issues that stress him, to either find ways of avoiding such stresses or develop life management skills to better cope with such demands; and to self-observe and recognize characteristic early behaviors or warning signals that indicate he is moving towards a repetition of his offense. Table 2 provides an overview of psychoeducational services regularly provided to inmates at the Connecticut Correctional Institution at Somers.

REHABILITATION

It would be misleading to suggest that we have reached a state of clinical knowledge that insures the successful rehabilitation of adults who sexually molest children. As yet, no single method of treatment or type of therapeutic intervention has proved to be a totally effective remedy. And given the wide range of individual differences found among child molesters, it is unlikely that any single treatment will ever prove suitable for all such offenders. Treatment has to be tailored to the specific needs and abilities of the individual client. Since, by definition, a sexual assault is an interpersonal act involving sexuality and aggression, at a minimum these three major issues (aggression, sexuality, and interpersonal relations) must be addressed in any program of treatment or rehabilitation.

In working with involuntary clients, treatment is necessarily compulsory and traditional approaches must be adapted or modified for this client. This includes exercising power over the client in a responsible fashion, confronting and controlling him, doing persistent outreach and monitoring, providing concrete support services, anticipating the guidance he needs, and implementing the consequences or penalities for failure to fulfill the conditions of treatment.

Our expectations of clients in treatment are that they will come to recognize their problems through knowledge of their symptoms, admit to their behavior, see it as inappropriate, realize it is compulsive behavior over which they must gain control, accept responsibility for what they have done, and make amendments. Basically, treatment is coercive—the offender, realizing the social and legal consequences of disclosure does not self-refer. Therefore, treatment must be confrontative. The client needs to be told that he has a problem and needs help and told where to get help.

Table 2: Application Form, Sex Offender Program, Connecticut Correctional Institution-Somers

Indicate your choices and their order of preference:

1. ( ) REGULAR GROUP THERAPY. (Members within the same group will all have committed a similar type of offense. Discussion will focus on your offense and the underlying issues related to it.)
2. ( ) SEX EDUCATION. (A basic introduction to human sexuality. Discussion will focus on myths about sex, common questions and concerns, variations in sexual behavior, values and attitudes. Attention will be given to sexual roles, gender and identity issues, communication problems, reproduction, etc.)
3. ( ) RELATIONSHIPS TO WOMEN. (Discussion will focus on concerns and problems experienced in relating to women. Attention will be given to attitudes toward women, expectations in regard to women, and an understanding of women's issues.)
4. ( ) PERSONAL VICTIMIZATION. (Discussion will focus on concerns and problems experienced in regard to having been a victim of abuse, trauma, or exploitation as a youngster or young adult. Attention will be given to better understand one's sexual and aggressive attitudes, values, fantasies, and the like, as well as to concerns and problems experienced in regard to sexual development.)
5. ( ) UNDERSTANDING SEXUAL ASSAULT. (Discussion will focus on the dynamics of sexual offenses, patterns of assault, the psychology of the offender, clinical aspects of sexual assault, treatment approaches, etc.)
6. ( ) VICTIM PERSONALIZATION. (Discussion will focus on the impact of various types of sexual offenses on the victim. Attention will be given to the aftereffects of sexual assault on victims, both male and female, adult and child. This group will help the offender to more fully understand and appreciate why victims behave as they do and how their lives are affected by being victimized.)
7. ( ) MANAGEMENT OF ANGER AND AGGRESSION. (Discussion will focus on difficulties in regard to aggression management, such as having a problem with one's temper, or getting involved in high

risk activities for excitement, and on efforts to better handle these feelings. Attention will be given to ways of being assertive without being aggressive and to the underlying reasons related to anger and aggression.)

8. ( ) SOCIODRAMA/COMMUNICATION SKILLS. (This group will focus on interrelating and communicating effectively with others. Through the use of role-playing and video-taping participants will be able to improve their empathy, social skills, and communications in dealing with life situations involving other people.)

9. ( ) COMBATTING SEXUAL ASSAULT. (At various times throughout the year different people who are concerned about sexual assault and interested in learning more about the sexual offender will visit the Sex Offender Program at CCI-Somers. They may be students, victim counselors, law enforcement officers, nurses, therapists, and the like, whose work brings them into contact with the victim of sexual assault, the offender, or both. Your knowledge and experience can contribute to their understanding and education.)

10. ( ) PARENTS ANONYMOUS. (Participation in this group is limited to men who are parents or are in a parenting relationship with one or more children. Parents Anonymous operates on the self-help, mutual-aid concept or model. Members of the group set agenda and decide how they wish to use group time. Major issues to be dealt with include how to be an effective parent, how to relate to children appropriately, etc.)

11. ( ) DEALING WITH ANXIETY AND TENSION: BIOFEEDBACK. (Focus is on learning to relax and relieve tension through an individual biofeedback process. The inmate uses a series of instructional tapes that teach him stress reduction and relaxation techniques and measures his progress on a biofeedback machine.)

Essentially there are two basic options in regard to disposition of child molestation cases: 1. the offender may be incarcerated or 2. the offender may be referred to an outpatient program or agency for treatment. In our view the latter should always be stipulated as a condition of probation or parole.

DISPOSITION GUIDELINES

In the assessment of the offender we find treatment in an outpatient setting counterindicated when:

a. the threat of harm or actual physical force or abuse played a role in the offense,

b. the sexual activity involved any bizarre or ritualistic acts (such as enemas or bondage),

c. the sexual offense is one aspect of numerous antisocial behaviors or a criminal lifestyle,

d. the sexual offense is secondary to a condition of serious psychopathology (such as psychosis, retardation, addiction, or organicity),
e. the offense constitutes a chronic sexual fixation on children rather than a regression under identifiable stresses,
f. the offender either denies his offense or does not regard such behavior as inappropriate and there is no dependable agent to supervise or monitor his daily living,
g. the offender has few psychological areas of conflict-free functioning and few dependable social and occupational skills to manage most adult demands adequately.

When some or most of the above conditions prevail, then the placement of choice is an institutional setting. However, whatever treatment is begun or accomplished in this setting must be continued on an outpatient basis after release.

Since in fact child molesters will be found in a variety of settings—in prisons, in mental hospitals, in residential treatment programs, and in the community—treatment services need to be available in all these settings. Furthermore, since we regard this problem as a chronic one, it is something the offender will need to work on every day of his life and there will need to be support services available to help him—not only professional agencies and programs, but also, and even more important, self-help groups such as Parents Anonymous, Parents United, Alcoholics Anonymous, and the like. Unfortunately, many mental health and social service agencies shy away from treating sexual offenders because of their discomfort over the nature of the behavior or because they feel they lack the expertise to counsel this group of individuals. Some agencies are willing to treat the offender, but do so in traditional ways which are often inappropriate and/or ineffective for this client. They may avoid discussing the actual offense, for example, because they are uncomfortable with the subject, whereas we feel that it is necessary to discuss and directly confront the behavior early on in treatment. Another problem centers around the issue of therapist-client confidentiality. Although confidentiality may be appropriate when treating non-criminal behavior, it is not appropriate when dealing with the child sex offender since it perpetuates the secrecy which is so much a part of the offense itself. The therapist must assume professional responsibility to protect any potential victims of this client.

SUMMARY

One of the crucial factors in combatting the sexual molestation of children is the identification and treatment of the offender. Yet most clinicians are not being trained to work with such clients in the course of their graduate schooling. As a result, offenders continue to be recycled back into the community without the support services necessary to reduce the risk of recidivism. In this chapter, we have attempted to provide an introductory overview of the child molester, to summarize our clinical impressions derived from many years work with such offenders, and to offer some guidelines and suggestions for assessing and treating such referrals. The aim of this chapter is not to provide anything approaching a definitive work on the child offender, but instead to offer a framework for human service providers who come into contact with such clients so as to facilitate their work in dealing with this complex and multidetermined issue.

To effect such treatment requires an inter-agency and multidisciplinary team approach. Child molestation is behavior that crosses clinical, legal, and social boundaries and to effectively combat this serious problem there must be open communication among all who play a role in the management of the offender—the clinician, the court, the parole or probation officer, the victim's counselor, and the like.

SUGGESTED READINGS

Burgess, A. W.; Groth, A. N.; H., L. L.; & Sgroi, S. M. *Sexual Assault of Children and Adolescents*, Lexington: Lexington Books, 1978.

Groth, A. N., with Birnbaum, H. J. *Men who Rape: The Psychology of the Offender*, New York: Plenum, 1979.

Sanford, L. T. *The Silent Children*, New York: Doubleday, 1980.

Sgroi, S. M. *A Handbook of Clinical Intervention in Child Sexual Abuse*, Lexington: Lexington Books, 1981.

Pedophilia: Diagnostic Concepts Treatment, and Ethical Considerations

Fred S. Berlin, M.D., Ph.D. and
Edgar Krout, M.A.

Over the past decade we have become increasingly aware of the extent and magnitude of the sexual victimization of children in our society and considerable efforts have been made to offer help and assistance to these victims. However, to a large extent, their perpetrators have been regarded more as offenders deserving punishment than as persons needing help.

This paper serves to broaden the base of our knowledge in regard to an adult's sexual attraction to a child and helps us differentiate between the perpetrator and his offense. It is a conceptual work, exploring the nature of pedophilia, its etiology, manifestation, diagnosis, and treatment which encompasses both clinical and ethical considerations.

To an issue fraught with myth, misconception, fear, hostility, and ignorance, Dr. Berlin and Mr. Krout's paper brings clarity, order, understanding, and hope. It is only through understanding and with understanding that we will find the way to help perpetrators inhibit unwanted pedophilic inclinations. The sexual victimiza-

Fred S. Berlin is Associate Professor, School of Medicine, Johns Hopkins University, Baltimore, Maryland. He is also Co-Director of The Johns Hopkins Hospital Sexual Disorders Clinic and a member of the American College of Forensic Psychiatry. Edgar W. Krout is a psychotherapist in the Department of Psychiatry at Johns Hopkins Hospital and a member of the staff of The Johns Hopkins Sexual Disorders Clinic. This article is reprinted from *American Journal of Forensic Psychiatry*, volume VII, issue 1, pp 13–30. The *Journal* is a publication of the American College of Forensic Psychiatry, 26701 Quail Creek, #295, Laguna Hills, CA 92656. Reprinted by permission of the publisher.

tion of children is the abuse of power. Knowledge is power, and through knowledge we are empowered to address this problem and make our society a safer one for our children. This paper is an important contribution to the sparse literature on a serious subject.

A. Nicholas Groth, Ph.D., Co-Director, Sex Offender Program
State of Connecticut Dept. of Correction, Somers State Prison

THE NATURE OF HUMAN SEXUALITY

People do not decide voluntarily what will arouse them sexually. Rather, in maturing they discover the nature of their own sexual orientation and interests. Persons differ from one another in terms of (a) the types of *partners* whom they find to be erotically appealing, and (b) the types of *behaviors* that they find to be erotically appealing. They also differ in intensity of sexual drive, the degree of difficulty that they experience in trying to resist sexual temptations, and in their attitudes about whether or not such temptations should be resisted.

When persons experience erotic desires to engage in types of sexual behaviors that could cause themselves or others harm, such as sadistic, coercive or masochistic sexual involvements, psychiatric help may be needed. This may also be necessary when a person experiences strong erotic attractions towards unacceptable sexual partners, such as children.

Some psychiatric diagnoses can be made, then, simply by asking cooperative persons about the range of behaviors they find to be erotically appealing and about the difficulty they experience in trying to resist succumbing to such sexual temptations. This line of questioning can identify the person who meets the DSM III diagnostic criteria for sexual exhibitionism, sexual sadism, sexual masochism, transvestism, and compulsive voyeurism (American Psychiatric Association, 1978). Each of these represents an unconventional form of sexual appetite. These men, unlike the average man, often experience great difficulty resisting erotic temptations to repeatedly expose themselves, to repeatedly have themselves beaten, or to repeatedly peep in windows, depending upon the nature of their particular sexual compulsion. Masturbation cannot fully satisfy these cravings because what they crave is not just sexual release, but a specific type of sexual activity. Thus, although the average man is physically capable of exposing himself publicly, he does not have to repeatedly fight off the urge to do so, as does the exhibitionist, in order to stay out of trouble.

Another way in which sexual problems possibly requiring psychiatric assistance can be identified is by inquiring about the range and types of *partners* that a person finds to be erotically appealing, and about how difficult it is to resist the temptation to become involved sexually with such partners. Some men, for example, report that they are attracted sexually to both children and adults, but that when they have a satisfying adult relationship they are able to resist the temptation of becoming sexually intimate with a child. Some such men, however, during periods of time in their lives when they do not have a satisfying adult relationship do become involved sexually with children. Groth (1979) refers to such men who find both adults and children to be erotically appealing as regressed pedophiles. There are other men who experience absolutely no erotic attraction whatsoever towards adults but who have a great deal of difficulty resisting the sexual temptations that they experience towards children. Groth refers to these men as fixated pedophiles.

Pedophilia then is simply a term used to indicate that an adult finds children to be sexually appealing. This condition seems to have been identified almost exclusively in men. If a man is attracted sexually only to boys, a diagnosis of homosexual pedophilia can be made, whereas if he is attracted only to girls, a diagnosis of heterosexual pedophilia may be in order. If gender is not a factor, then the appropriate diagnosis is bisexual pedophilia. As with other appetites, the pedophilic appetite craves satiation, with recurrence of hunger an expected event.

Some men who are attracted sexually to children desire not to be and would like to change. Under such circumstances, their sexual attractions to children are said to be ego-dystonic. If a man's sexual attraction towards children does not conflict with his conscience and personal moral convictions, then his pedophilic desires are said to be ego-syntonic. In very rare instances, some men experience erotically sadistic desires towards children. Under such circumstances, a diagnosis of sexual sadism should also be made.

There are some men who find children to be somewhat appealing erotically but who, nevertheless, find it easy to resist becoming sexually involved. Such persons may not require professional assistance. Those who do experience difficulty resisting such temptations on their own, however, may require help.

The following is a brief verbatim quote from a man whose sexual orientation can be characterized as ego-dystonic, fixated, homosexual pedophilic. The comments of this patient give some sense of how tortured and conflicted he feels by the sexual lusts and cravings that he experiences towards young boys:

> What starts a person like myself doing what I do? Why me? Why can't I be normal like everybody else? You know, did God put this as a punishment or something towards me? I am ashamed. Why can't I just go out and have a good time with girls? I feel empty when a female is present. An older 'gay' person would turn me off. I have thought about suicide. I think after this long period of time, I have actually seen where I have an illness. It is getting uncontrolla-

ble to the point where I can't put up with it anymore. It is a sickness. I know it's a sickness. But as far as society is concerned, you are a criminal and should be punished. Even if I go to jail for twelve or fifteen years, or whatever, I am still going to be the same when I get out.

This last statement was not meant to be defiant.

ETIOLOGY OF PEDOPHILIC SEXUAL DESIRES

It is a deeply rooted aspect of human nature that we experience desires to seek out a partner with whom we can share tenderness, affection, companionship, and physical intimacy. Even in animals, one can observe the so-called mating instinct. People do not experience feelings of erotic love because it is intellectually rational to do so, or because they have been taught that it is sensible to do so. Rather, there is a certain "chemistry" involved. Most of us can describe attributes, both physical and psychological, that comprise our archetypical fantasies of an idealized partner or mate. In the overwhelming majority of cases, the object of our erotic affections is a peer. Most adults do not (1) become involved sexually with children, (2) repeatedly fantasize about children when masturbating, (3) find pictures of naked children more erotic than pictures of naked adults, and (4) have to repeatedly fight off the temptation of becoming involved with children in a sexual or romantic way.

In addition to yearning for a loving adult sexual relationship, almost all of us are aware of the fact that infants and children often elicit an emotional response from us. Rather than involving feelings of lust or erotic love, however, the feelings which often well up internally in response to children are ordinarily ones of affection and gentleness, as well as a desire to nurture, cherish, and protect. It is sometimes difficult to resist the urge to pick up and cuddle a young infant or child. We do not ordinarily fall in love with children, however, in a romantic or sexual way.

Most young people devote a great deal of time, thought, and energy towards seeking out a partner with whom to share affection, companionship, and physical intimacy. The man who, for unknown reasons, discovers that he craves that type of relationship with a child rather than with an adult, however, copes with life from a very different perspective.

Some have argued that sexual assaults are invariably aggressive (Groth, 1979). In the vast majority of pedophilic acts, this is simply not so. Most pedophiles use no physical force whatsoever, but instead derive pleasure from engaging in sexual activities with children, sometimes in a caring way (Baker et al, 1968; Berlin, 1983b). By definition, the issue to be explained in pedophilia is one of sexual and affectional orientation. Pedophilia is not a disturbance of temperament or aggression.

SEXUAL ORIENTATION: PENECTOMIZED MALE REARED AS A GIRL

How is it then that sexual orientation and affectional interests are acquired? It appears that both life experience and constitution play a role. The role that environment can play was dramatically demonstrated by a tragic case reported by Money (1980) in which one of two genetically identical male twins was so severely damaged at the time of circumcision several months after birth that a total penectomy was required. That child was then reared as a girl. The child's chromosomal pattern, of course, remained unchanged, and she has now reached her teenaged years. She has developed breasts by virtue of having been administered estrogens; surgically, an artificial vagina has been created. According to Diamond (1982), however, she nevertheless experiences considerable difficulty in adjusting as a female, and she is in some ways ambivalent about her status. Still, at age 19, this twin raised as a female apparently feels herself to be a woman in terms of gender identity and also experiences some level of sexual attraction towards age-appropriate males. Thus, although she is a woman with an XY rather than a XX chromosomal karyotype, as a consequence presumably of how she has been raised, she feels herself to be a woman and she finds men to be sexually appealing.

MANY PEDOPHILES FORMER "VICTIMS"

There are many additional examples showing that environment and life experiences can play at least some role in the development of gender identity and in the development of sexual orientation and interest. Groth (1979) and others have shown that many men who experience pedophilic erotic urges as adults were sexually involved with adults when they were children. Thus, in treating the pedophile one is in point of fact often treating a former "victim." One is merely treating him later on in his life after the circumstances of his childhood, or the intricacies of his biological constitution, have produced their psychological sequelae. Why sexual involvements with an adult during childhood seem to put some at risk of experiencing pedophilic sexual urges later on in life, but not others, is not known.

Money (1980) has proposed that excessive prohibition of early sexual expression may also put one at risk of developing pedophilic sexual desires. He has reported that many men with sexual disorders have come from homes where even the slightest expression of sexuality, including masturbation, was severely chastised. Gaffney et al (1984a) has documented evidence that pedophilia may occur more frequently within certain families.

Biology, too, can play a role in the development of sexual interests. Sexual behavior in humans is often a response to subjectively experienced erotic desires and fantasies. Although it appears that specific sexual tastes or preferences may sometimes be modified by virtue of early life experiences, the phenomenon of sexual desire itself is apparently unlearned and rooted in biology. Males do not have to be taught how to obtain an erection. Just as it is true of language and dialect, once acquired sexual desires are not readily modified.

It is just as reasonable to ask whether one might be put at risk of developing unconventional sexual interests, such as pedophilia, by virtue of the presence of certain biological abnormalities, as it is reasonable to ask whether one could be put at such risk by being exposed early on in life to certain environmental events. One way of addressing this issue would be to try to determine whether or not there is an increased prevalence of biological abnormalities of the sort thought to be related to human sexuality among a group of men who experience unconventional sexual interests.

BIOLOGICAL ABNORMALITIES

Berlin (1983b) evaluated 41 men, all of whom met the DSM III diagnostic criteria for some form of paraphilia ("sexual deviation disorder") looking for the possible presence of biological abnormalities. The majority of these men were either pedophiles or exhibitionists. Although no significant abnormalities were detected in 12 of the 41, a total of 63 abnormalities was found among the other 29 men. These included 7 chromosomal anomalites (most frequently Klinefelter's syndrome), as well as 18 abnormal levels of testosterone, 8 of follicle stimulating hormone, and 14 of luteinizing hormone. There were also 7 abnormal CT scans of the brain, 4 pathological EEG's, and 5 abnormal neurological examinations. Following statistical analysis, Berlin (1983b) concluded, as have others, that there may, indeed, be an association between the presence of certain kinds of biological abnormalities and the presence of unconventional kinds of sexual interests such as pedophilia. Recently, Gaffney and Berlin (1984) documented an abnormal pattern of luteinizing hormone (LH) release over time in response to the intravenous administration of bolus of luteinizing hormone releasing factor (LHRF) in a group of pedophilic patients. At The Johns Hopkins Hospital Sexual Disorders Clinic, it is unusual to see a man who experiences recurrent pedophilic cravings in the absence of (a) a significant biological abnormality, (b) a past history of sexual involvements with an adult during childhood, or (c) both.

ASSESSMENT: DISTINGUISHING BETWEEN (1) DIMINISHED MENTAL CAPACITIES, (2) PERSONALITY TRAITS, AND (3) SEXUAL ORIENTATION

Persons are sometimes referred for psychiatric evaluation because they have become sexually involved with a child. However, a diagnosis such as pedophilia cannot be made simply by considering behavior alone. Rather, for purposes of diagnosis and for proper treatment, one must try to appreciate the state of mind which contributed to the individual's behavior.

Like any behavior, sexual behavior with a child can be enacted for a variety of reasons. For example, a person with schizophrenia may behave in a particular way in response to hallucinations "telling him to do so," whereas the alcoholic's behavior may be a reflection of diminished judgment secondary to intoxication. A mentally retarded individual may become involved sexually with a child (who incidentally may be of the same approximate mental age as he) because of the lack of availability of adult partners, and a lack of capacity to fully appreciate and understand the wrongful nature of his actions. In none of these instances would a primary diagnosis of pedophilia necessarily apply.

In DSM II, conditions such as pedophilia used to be considered subcategories of a specific personality type (i.e., the so-called antisocial personality disorder). DSM III (APA, 1978) acknowledges that this is by no means necessarily so. Diagnosing a person as a pedophile says something about the nature of his sexual desires and orientation. It says nothing whatsoever, however, about his temperament, or about traits of character (such as kindness versus cruelty, caring versus uncaring, sensitive versus insensitive, and so on). Thus, a diagnosis of pedophilia does not necessarily mean that a person is lacking in conscience, diminished in intellectual capabilities, or somehow "characterologically flawed." In evaluating a person who has become sexually involved with a child, one needs to try to determine whether the behavior in question was a reflection of (a) psychosis, (b) poor judgment and psychological immaturity, (c) lack of conscience, (d) diminished intellect, (e) intoxication, (f) a pedophilic sexual orientation, or (g) a combination of these plus other factors. One needs to evaluate independently, the nature of an individual's sexual drives and interests, as opposed to what that person is like in terms of character, intellect, temperament, and other mental capacities.

PEDOPHILIC BEHAVIOR AND ITS RELATIONSHIP TO HUMAN APPETITES AND COMPULSIONS

Although, in order to hold persons accountable for their own actions, society tends to presume that individuals can invariably control their own behavior through "willpower" alone, this is simply not always so (Carnes, 1983). It is easy for a nonsmoker to argue that any smoker could stop if he or she really wanted to do so. Surely, this must be so in the case of the pregnant smoker, if not for her sake, then certainly for the sake of not abusing her unborn child. Many of those who have tried to give up smoking and failed, however, can appreciate the difficulty involved in trying to overcome that habit.

Patients on kidney dialysis made thirsty by the procedure often have great difficulty maintaining necessary fluid restrictions, even though not doing so can be life threatening to them (Wirth and Folstein, 1982). The more thirsty they are made by the procedure, the more difficulty they experience in limiting fluid intake. The researchers who documented this finding concluded that limits to fluid intake set by physicians may not suffice because they differ from those set by the patient's own physiology (Wirth and Folstein, 1982).

It is easy for a person who is not tempted sexually by children to argue that any pedophile could stop having sex with children if he would simply make up his mind to do so. Admittedly, sometimes it is difficult to determine whether a person is trying his/her best and failing, or just not trying. This does not mean, though, that many are not trying. When it comes to appetites or drives such as hunger, thirst, pain, the need for sleep or for sex, biological regulatory systems exist that may cause an individual to experience desires to satisfy those hungers in ways that cannot invariably be successfully resisted through willpower alone. Sometimes persons may feel so discomforted by their cravings that they feel compelled to act in order to diminish their discomfort.

A common source of confusion about whether or not persons can control compulsive or appetite-related behaviors, such as pedophilia, relates to the observation that often such behaviors are enacted in a premeditated fashion. A pedophile rarely approaches a child, for example, when a policeman is present. It is important to appreciate, however, that this is not unlike the case of the cigarette smoker who may be able to *temporarily* refrain from smoking while in his doctor's office because his physician's presence causes a feeling to well up inside which helps him to control his behavior. This does not mean that that smoker will necessarily be able to break the smoking habit, though, when his efforts to do so depend not upon the stabilizing presence of another individual but upon his willpower alone.

A major issue in trying to understand human behavior relates to whether one should consider a person to be (a) the passive product of life experience and constitution, *versus* (b) a conscious agent capable of transcending prior determinants. One does not want to excuse as "psychopathology" irresponsible behavior. On the other hand, one should not be too quick to label as misbehavior the compulsive sexual acts of persons needing help in order to be able to better control their behavior. Often a double standard is applied in dealing with compulsive paraphilic types of human sexuality. If a person states that he is trying his best to diet, to stop smoking, or to stop compulsive handwashing, he is often believed and helped. If, however, a person says he needs help in order to be able to resist the urge to have sex with children, to expose himself publically, or to engage in coercive sexual acts, his claim that he cannot control himself through willpower alone is often dismissed. In the authors' judgment, many men with pedophilic sexual orientations do need help in order to be able to control their behavior appropriately.

TREATMENT OF PEDOPHILIA: CONCEPTUAL CONSIDERATIONS

Four major modalities have been proposed for treating pedophilia. They are (1) psychotherapy, (2) behavior therapy, (3) surgery, and (4) medication.

Psychotherapy

Classic psychodynamic theory *assumes* that all men would ordinarily develop conventional erotic attractions towards age-appropriate partners of the opposite sex, but that this does not occur in some instances because unhealthy early life experiences interferred with the normal process of psychological maturation. Therapy utilizes the process of introspection to try to figure out what went wrong, with the expectation that newly acquired insights will then facilitate the problem being rectified.

It is doubtful that individuals can come to fully understand the basis of their own sexual interests through the process of introspection alone. The average man probably cannot figure out simply by thinking about it why he prefers women rather than men. Similarly, it is not certain that the pedophilic individual can figure out the basis of his own sexuality. Furthermore, even if he could, knowing why one is hungry—be it for food or for children, doesn't make one any less hungry, nor does it make it any easier for one to resist temptation. Finally, there is little convincing evidence showing that the traditional psychotherapies alone are an effective means for treating pedophilia.

Behavior Therapy

Behavior therapists tend to be less concerned with the historical antecedents of pedophilia than with the question of what can be done about it. The feature common to most behavioral approaches is an attempt to extinguish erotic feelings associated with children, while simultaneously teaching an individual to become sexually aroused by formerly non-arousing age-appropriate partners. Although in laboratory situations, behaviorists have shown that some pedophilic men no longer demonstrate physiological evidence of sexual arousal when looking at pictures of naked children, and that they can begin to show arousal to age-appropriate stimuli, it has *not* been well established that such changes invariably carry over into the non-laboratory situation (Marks, 1981). Most of us can appreciate how difficult it would be to try and stop feeling the sexual attractions we have experienced as natural throughout our lives. There is no reason to believe that it is any easier for the fixated homosexual pedophile to learn to lose his interest in boys and to become sexually aroused by women, than it would be for the average male to lose his interest in women and to instead begin lusting for young boys.

Punishment

Another type of "behavior therapy" that has been tried is punishment, usually in the form of incarceration. Although society sometimes chooses to punish for reasons other than behavior modification, behavior modification is often one of the intended goals. There is however nothing about being in prison that can change the nature of a pedophile's sexual orientation or that can increase his ability to resist acting upon improper sexual temptations.

Surgery

Two types of surgery have been proposed as a treatment for pedophilia. They are (1) sterotactic neurosurgery, and (2) removal of the testes. Neurosurgery for this purpose is still investigational and will not be discussed here. Its rationale has been explored in a review article by Freund (1980).

Removal of the testes (castration) has been suggested as a treatment for pedophilia because the testes are the major source of testosterone production in the body. There has been much confusion about castration, a procedure which does not remove the penis, but which instead removes the testes in order to lower testosterone.

Testosterone is an important hormone related to human sexuality and gender differences. If the testes of a male fail to produce adequate amounts during early embryonic life, he will be born with the external anatomical appearance of a female. Thus, testosterone causes external anatomical masculinization of the fetus, and also produces certain changes in the endocrinological functioning of the male brain (Witson et al, 1981). The marked increase in testosterone production which occurs at the time of puberty in males is associated with the development of increased pubic and facial hair, deepening of the voice, an increase of muscle mass, and a marked increase in sexual libido. The idea of lowering testosterone in the case of the pedophile is to try to decrease the intensity of his sexual cravings, which are for children.

Some critics have argued that castrating the "sex offender," which involves removal of the testes, and not the penis, is like cutting off the hand of the thief. This is in no way so. Cutting off the penis would be analogous to cutting off the hand of the thief. A male animal whose penis has been surgically removed will still try to mount a female in heat, suggesting that the penectomized male is still sexually motivated, though unable sexually to perform. A castrated male, on the other hand, whose penis is intact can perform sexually but will ordinarily not attempt to mount a female in heat, suggesting that he is no longer motivated to do so.

In animals, lowering testosterone by means of removing the testes usually eventually leads to a total cessation of virtually all sexually motivated behavior, although sometimes this may take as long as two years to occur (Freund, 1980). In humans, the relationship between very low testosterone levels and low sexual libido is also fairly well established. This evidence comes from a variety of sources including studies on hypogonadal men, data from persons with adrenogenital disorders, studies on drugs that lower testosterone as side effects, and from several well controlled studies looking at the effects of administering testosterone in an attempt to increase sexual libido (Ellis, 1982; Kwan et al, 1983; Sturup, 1972; Carney et al, 1978).

THERAPEUTIC SEX DRIVE REDUCTION

In an article entitled, "Therapeutic Sex Drive Reduction," Freund (1980) reviewed data regarding removal of the testes in humans as a means of trying to help some men gain better control over their sexual behavior. In one study in Denmark, Sturup (1972) reported upon a thirty-year investigation of 900 castrated "sex offenders," many of whom were pedophiles, involving over 4,000 follow-up examinations. He documented less than a 3 percent recidivism rate. Ficher Van Rossum in Holland, Kinmark and Oster in Sweden, and

Cornu in Switzerland reported comparable findings (Freund, 1980). The study in Holland involved 237 men with a 1.3 percent recidivism.

In the Swiss study, there was a 5.8 percent recidivism rate among 120 men following castration, with a 52 percent recidivism rate in the noncastrated control group. Follow-ups ranged from five to thirty years. Bremmer (1959) reported a 58 percent recidivism rate in the five years prior to treatment, in a group of men who showed only a 7.3 percent recidivism rate during the five years post-surgery. Thus, the surgical method of lowering testosterone did seem to enable many men to better control their sexual behaviors. Furthermore, many of these men did not lose their capacity to perform sexually following castration.

CYPROTERONE ACETATE AND MEDROXYPROGESTERONE ACETATE

Today it is no longer necessary to perform castration in order to reduce testosterone levels. Rather, this can now be done pharmacologically in a graduated way without the physical or psychological trauma of surgery. In Europe and the Scandinavian countries, cyproterone acetate has been used for this purpose, and there are several "blind" as well as "non-blind" studies supporting its effectiveness (Laschet and Laschet, 1976; Money et al, 1976). In the United States, since Money first began doing so in 1967 in conjunction with the treatment of pedophilia, the drug most often employed as a pharmocological method for lowering testosterone has been medroxyprogesterone acetate, Depo-Provera (Money et al, 1976; Berlin & Meinecke, 1981; Berlin & Coyle, 1981; Berlin, 1981; Berlin & Schaerf, 1984).

Medroxyprogesterone acetate (MPA) can be injected intramuscularly once per week. There it binds to the muscle, from where it is then gradually released over the course of several days into the blood stream. At this time, the initial starting dosage used in The Johns Hopkins Clinic has been 500mg IM once per week of the 100mg per cc concentration. No more than 250cc is given into a single injection site.

Major side effects of MPA have been weight gain, and in some cases hypertension. Mild lethergy, cold sweats, nightmares, hot flashes, and muscle aches have also been reported. The drug, which is not feminizing, may cause an increased incidence of breast cancer in female beagle dogs, and of uterine cancer in monkeys. It has been used in over eighty countries of the world as a female contraceptive, supported in its use for this purpose by the World Health Organization. No studies showing an increased risk of cancer in males (either humans or animals) have been reported. Two recent articles, one in *Science* (Sun. 1982) and the other in *The Journal of the American Medical Association* (Rosenfield et al, 1983), failed to find convincing evidence that MPA is carcinogenic in humans.

There is no doubt that MPA consistently decreases serum testosterone levels significantly. This can be confirmed by means of a simple blood test. The idea of using MPA in the case of the pedophile is to try to decrease the intensity of his sexual cravings, thereby, hopefully, making it easier for him to successfully resist unwanted temptations. The drug cannot change the nature of his sexual orientation.

What is not yet fully established regarding the use of MPA is optimal dosage, which of the paraphilias will respond most adequately, long-term side effects, and precise long-term recidivism percentages. There is little reason to believe, however, that recidivism should be any higher than those low rates documented when surgical removal of the testes was used as a method of lowering testosterone. Of more than 70 men treated at The Johns Hopkins Clinic with MPA over the past three years for some form of paraphilia (mostly pedophilia and exhibitionism), less than 10 percent have relapsed. In addition, compliance rates have been better than 90 percent.

There has been some concern about whether MPA should be given to pedophilic men who are on legal probation. In the author's opinion, if it is not an effective drug, then it should not be used at all. If it is effective, as it often seems to be, then it is difficult to see why a person should be denied the opportunity to take it just because he is on probation or perhaps even incarcerated. Some incarcerated men report that MPA frees them from intrusive, obsessional sexual preoccupations.

MPA is not a cure. It is not a guarantee. It is not a punishment. Some pedophiles report being unable to successfully resist sexual temptations through willpower alone, even with the assistance of professional counseling. Such individuals should be afforded the opportunity to see whether or not MPA confers upon them an increased capacity for self-control.

RATIONALE FOR USE OF MPA PLUS COUNSELING

Some critics have argued that psychotropic drugs such as MPA may in some ways be "mind controlling." The legitimate medical indications for use of psychotropic drugs are (a) to decrease suffering (as in the case of antidepressant medications), (b) to restore function (as in the case of "antipsychotic medications"), or (c) to increase rather than decrease a person's capacity to successfully exercise self-control as in the case of MPA (Berlin, 1983a).

Most pedophiles receiving MPA also attend group counseling sessions. These are similar to the type often used with alcoholics. There they are expected to acknowledge being tempted to do something improper. They then discuss among themselves strategies intended to help enable them to resist such temptations successfully. This includes discussions of whom to call, what early warning signs to look for, and what situations to avoid. The groups provide both peer pressure and peer support.

When a person desires sex or falls in love, it is often easy to become convinced that the relationship is good and healthy and not harmful or wrong. Such self-deception may at times be easy for the pedophilic individual in light of the fact that sex with children, though wrong, may not in every instance be damaging (Standfort, 1984). Some children may enjoy certain sexual and non-sexual aspects of their relationships with an adult, thus facilitating self-deception on the part of the adult. Treatment, therefore, may have to involve helping a person stop rationalizing, as well as helping him to develop strategies for more successfully resisting sexual and affectional temptations.

ETHICAL CONSIDERATIONS AND CONCLUDING COMMENTS

A few hundred years ago in New England, misguided parishioners burned at the stake women whose behaviors they feared or found offensive. Persons whom we might now treat in psychiatric hospitals were shackled, often for the better part of a life time. In the 1700s, the most common cause for execution in the British Royal Navy was the crime of "buggery," homosexual behavior between consenting adults (Gilbert, 1976). In each of these instances, many good people failed to appreciate the wrongful nature of these reactions. Today, the person with a pedophilic sexual orientation is often ridiculed, maligned and disparaged, with little concern about him as a person. It is simply taken for granted that the pedophile is deserving of scorn, with little more thought given to such a proposition than was given several hundred years ago to the notion that lepers should be exiled. It is difficult contemporarily to be fully aware of one's own society's assumptions.

Today, most of us would probably accept as a given the belief that any man who becomes sexually intimate with a child must simply be a callous predator, unwilling to reflect upon the possibility that such an individual might have a genuine concern for the well being of children. Labels such as "molester" and "abuser" are readily applied with little forethought. After all, how could anyone who really cares about a child's well being show so little concern and manifest such an abuse of trust as to become sexually involved? There can be little doubt that children are too unprepared and too vulnerable to fully appreciate the consequences of sexual involvement with an adult. However, imagine what life must be like for the man who finds that he never experiences feelings of erotic arousal or romantic love towards adults, as much as he might wish that he could, but who recurrently lusts for or falls in love with young boys or girls in an erotic, sensual way.

To provide treatment to persons with pedophilic sexual orientations in no way reflects a lack of concern for young children. One can treat children and treat pedophiles as well. These are not mutually exclusive choices. In counseling a child, it may help if that child understands that the pedophilic individual may genuinely have cared about him, even though that caring was expressed in an improper way. Preventive treatment cannot be completely accomplished without dealing with the pedophile himself. To the extent that treatment helps the pedophile gain better self-control, both his interests and society's interests are well served.

Although it is not the pedophile's fault that he has the sexual orientation that he has, it is his responsibility to deal with his sexuality in a manner that does not put innocent children at risk. However, in order for him to be able to do this and to be held accountable by society, adequate treatment facilities must be made available, facilities where a person can seek help without fear of stigmatization, ridicule, retaliation, or unwarranted disdain. Only under such circumstances, can one expect an individual to talk candidly about the innermost aspects of his own sexuality. This requires trust.

The values that we try to instill in our children are important. Almost two thousand years ago as an outraged crowd attempted to stone to death a woman whose sexual behavior they considered offensive, one man stepped forward to stop the retribution, speaking against such revenge while espousing values such as compassion, understanding, forgiveness, and reformation. He asked that persons be judged not simply by their behavior but with some appreciation for their humanity. Perhaps that message still goes unheeded today when it comes to the issue of how we deal with some of those who have sexual and affectional orientations of a sort that frighten us, and that differ from our own.

REFERENCES

American Psychiatric Association (1978). *Diagnostic and Statistical Manual of Mental Disorders, 3rd Edition.* Task Force on Nomenclature and Statistics of American Psychiatric Association, Washington, D.C.

Baker, H. J. and Stoller, J. (1968). Can a biological force contribute to gender identity? *Amer. J. Psychiat.* 124:1653–1658.

Berlin, F. S. (1981). Ethical use of antiandrogenic medications. *Amer. J. Psychiat.* 138:1516–1517.

Berlin, F. S. (1983). Ethical use of psychiatric diagnosis. *Psychiat. Annals.* 13:231–331.

Berlin, F. S. (1983). Sex offenders: A biomedical perspective and a status report on biomedical treatment. In Greer, J. C. and Stuart, I. R. (Eds.), *The Sexual Aggressor: Current Perspectives on Treatment*, Van Nostrand Reinhold Company, New York.

Berlin, F. S. and Coyle, G. S. (1981). Sexual deviation syndromes. *The Johns Hopkins Med. J.* 149:119–125.

Berlin, F. S. and Meinecke, C. F. (1981). Treatment of sex offenders with antiandrogenic medication: Conceptualization, review of treatment modalities, and preliminary findings. *Amer. J. Psychiat.* 138:601–607.

Berlin, F. S. and Schaerf, F. W. (1985). Laboratory assessment of the paraphilias and their treatment with antiandrogenic medication. In Hall, R. C. W. and Bereseford, T. P., *A Handbook of Psychiatric Diagnostic Procedures*, Spectrum Publications, New York.

Bremer, J. (1959). *Asexualization: A Follow-Up Study of 244 Cases.* Macmillan, New York.

Carnes, P. (1983). *Sexual Addiction.* CompCare Publications, Minneapolis.

Carney, A., Bancroft, J., and Mathews, A. (1978). A combination of hormonal and psychological treatment for female sexual unresponsiveness: A comparative study. *Brit. J. Psychiat.* 132:339–346.

Cooper, A. J. (1981). A placebo-controlled trial of the antiandrogen cyproterone acetate in deviant hypersexuality. *Compreh. Psychiat.* 22:458–465.

Diamond, M. (1982). Sexual identity: Monzygotic twins reared in discordant sex roles and a BBC followup. *Arch. Sex. Behav.* 11:181–186.

Ellis, L. (1982). Developmental androgen fluctuations and the five dimensions of mammalian sex (with emphasis upon the behavioral dimension and the human species). *Etiol. & Sociobiol.* 3:171–197.

Freund, K. (1980). Therapeutic sex drive reduction. *Acta Psychiat. Scandinavica* (supplement) 287:1–39.

Gaffney, G. S. and Berlin, F. S. (1984). Is there a hypothalamic-pituitary-gonadal dysfunction in paedophilia? *Brit. J. Psychiat.* 145–657–660.

Gaffney, G. S., Berlin, F. S., and Lurie, S. F. (1984). Is there familial transmission of pedophilia? *J. Nervous & Mental Diseases* 172–546–548.

Gilbert, A. N. (1976). Buggery and the British Royal Navy 1700–1761. *J. Soc. Hist.* 10:72–76.

Groth, A. N. (1979). Sexual trauma in the life histories of rapists and child molesters. *Victimology: An International Journal* 4:10–16.

Kwan, M., Greenleaf, W. J., Mann, J., Crapo, L., and Davidson, J. M. (1933). The nature of androgen action on male sexuality: A combined laboratory—self report study on hypogonadal man. *J. Clin. Edocrinol. & Metabol.* 57:557–562.

Laschet, V. and Laschet, L. (1976). Antiandrogens in the treatment of sexual deviation in men. *J. Steroid Biochem.* 16:821–826.

Marks, I. M. (1981). Review of behavioral psychotherapy, II: Sexual disorders. *Amer. J. Psychiat.* 138:750–756.

Money, J. (1980). *Love and Love Sickness,* The Johns Hopkins University Press, Baltimore.

Money, J., Wideking, Walker, P. S., and Gain, D. (1976). Combined antiandrogenic and counselling program for treatment of 46 XY and 47 XYY sex offenders. In Sachar, E. J. (Ed.), *Hormones, Behavior and Psychopathology,* Raven Press, New York.

Rosenfield, A., Marne, D., Rochat, R., Shelton, J., and Hatcher, R. A. (1983). The Food and Drug Administration and medroxyprogesterone acetate: What are the issues? *JAMA* 249:2922–2928.

Sandfort, T. G. M. (1984). Sex in pedophilic relationships: An empirical investigation among a nonrepresentative group of boys. *J. Sex. Res.* 20:123–142.

Sturup, G. K. (1972). Castration: The total treatment. In Resnick, H. P. L. and Wolfgang, M.D. (Eds.), *Sexual Behaviors: Social, Clinical, and Legal Aspects,* Little Brown, Boston.

Sun, M. (1982). Depo-Provera debate revs up at FDA. *Science* 217:424–428.

Witson, J. D., George, F. W., and Griffin, J. E. (1981). The hormonal control of sexual development. *Science* 211:1278–1284.

Wirth, J. B. and Folstein, M. F. (1982). Thirst and weight gain during maintenance hemodialysis. *Psychosomatics* 23:1125–1134.

APPENDICES

Appendix A:
Selected Printed Materials

The following selective bibliography is divided into two sections. The first lists printed materials for use by, or with, children; the second lists materials for use by adults. The items listed were chosen because they give a positive, common sense approach to the topic and would prove helpful to children.

FOR CHILDREN AND YOUNG ADULTS

Abby, My Love (1985) Fiction, Middle/High School
  Irving Hadley
  Atheneum, NY
  Abby's boyfriend recounts his courtship days with her, and how, in a sensitive, caring way, he helps her to find the courage to disclose the sexual abuse that has marred her life.

Alice Doesn't Babysit Anymore (1985) Primary
  Kevin McGovern, MD
  Privately Published
  Storybook format educates children on how to avoid abuse from baby-sitters and other authority figures. Available from Alternatives to Sexual Abuse, Box 25537, Portland, OR 97225.

Amazing Spider-Man and Power Pack (1984) Intermediate/Middle
  NCPCA in cooperation with Marvel Comics Spider-Man teaches lessons on how to protect yourself from sexual abuse. Available from National Committee for Prevention of Child Abuse, 332 S Michigan Ave, Suite 1250, Chicago, IL 60604.

Annie: Once I Was a Little Bit Frightened (1983)
  Becky Montgomery and others
  Annie's story of uncomfortable touching by a neighbor can be used in aiding sexual abuse victims to tell about their abuse. Available from Rape and Abuse Crisis Center, PO Box 1655, Fargo, ND 58107.

A Better Safe than Sorry Book (1984) Preschool/Primary
  Sol and Judith Gordon
  Ed-U Press Inc., Fayetteville, NY
  This book, for parents to use with children, discusses good and bad

touching in words children can understand. Parent's guide stresses the importance of open communication with children on sexuality.

The Bluest Eye (1970) Fiction, Middle/High School
Toni Morrison
Washington Square Press
An 11-year-old black girl's story of rape by her father will aid incest victims in realizing that others have experienced similar trauma.

Daddy's Girl (1982) Fiction, High School
Charlotte Vale Allen
Berkley
A young girl's incestuous childhood is recounted.

Dear Elizabeth: The Diary of an Adolescent Victim of Sexual Abuse (1984) Fiction, Middle/High School
Helen Swan and Gene Mackey
Brenda's struggle to deal with molestation at the hands of her father is revealed. Available from Children's Institute of Kansas City, 9412 High Dr, Leawood, KS 66206.

Father's Days: A True Story of Incest (1981) Fiction, High School
Katherine Brady
Dell
The story of a young girl's incestuous childhood is told in hopes of breaking through the psychological isolation incest victims often experience.

Feeling Safe, Feeling Strong (1984) Intermediate/Middle
Susan Terkel and Janet E. Rench
Lerner Publications, MN
Using case histories interspersed with facts about sexual abuse, this book offers common sense advice on how to prevent sexual abuse and how to handle it if it has occurred.

Foster Child (1977) Fiction, Middle/High School
Marion Bauer
Seabury Press, NY
Renny, living in a foster home, is threatened by the sexual advances of Pop Beck. This fires her determination to save herself and the other children living there.

Frances Ann Speaks Out: My Father Raped Me (1977) Fiction, Intermediate & Up
Helen Chetin
New Seed Press
This book will lend support in a time of need to any child who has experienced the trauma of rape.

Good Hugs and Bad Hugs: How Can You Tell? (1985) Preschool
Angela R. Carl
Standard Publishing, Cincinnati, OH
Through the use of this activity book, preschoolers can learn personal safety.

It's My Body (No Date) Preschool/Primary
Lory Freeman
Parenting Press, Seattle, WA
Situations are depicted to help teach children the difference between appropriate and inappropriate touching and the action to take if problems arise. Parents' guide also available.

Liking Myself (1977) Preschool/Primary
Pat Palmer
Impact Publishers, San Luis Obispo, CA
Young children are introduced to the ideas of self-worth, assertiveness, and feelings.

The Mouse, the Monster and Me! (1977) Intermediate
Pat Palmer
Impact Publishers, San Luis Obispo, CA
Personal rights and responsibilities are taught through the vehicles of mild mice and aggressive monsters.

My Body Is Private (1984) Primary
Linda W. Girard
Albert Whitman & Co., Niles, IL
Builds a context of acceptable touching versus unacceptable touching. Emphasizes the child's right to say no. Includes notes to parents on how to use the book.

Never Say Yes to a Stranger (1985) Preschool through Middle
Susan Newman
Putman, NY
Designed to be read by adults to children, this book concentrates on teaching awareness.

No More Secrets for Me (1984) Intermediate
Oralee Wachter
Little
A child's right to say no and the concept of a trusted adult are emphasized in these four stories of children who find themselves in exploitive situations.

Private Zone: A Book Teaching Children Sexual Assault Prevention Tools (1982) Preschool/Primary
Frances Dayee
Warner Books
Acceptable touching by appropriate people is the theme of Dayee's book. A child's right to privacy is discussed. A parent's guide gives information about sexual assault.

Red Flag, Green Flag People (1983, rev. ed.) Preschool/Primary
Joy Williams
A coloring book teaches about the different kinds of touching and shows children what measures to take if touching becomes inappropriate. Available from Rape and Abuse Crisis Center, PO Box 1655, Fargo, ND 58107.

Safety Zone (1984) Primary
Linda D. Meyer
The Charles Franklin Press, Edmonds, WA
This booklet, designed for parents to use with children, offers tips to

avoid abduction in a nonthreatening context. Includes a section for parents. Available from The Charles Franklin Press, 18409 90th Ave, Edmonds, WA 98020.

Sexual Abuse: Let's Talk About It (1984) Intermediate & Up
Margaret O. Hyde
Westminster
This book defines sexual abuse, gives children a course of action to follow, exonerates any feelings of guilt they may harbor, tells them where to go for help, and outlines what will happen when they do.

Some Questions You May Ask about Going to Court
Kids Go to Court Too
Two pamphlets designed to prepare children and parents for court. Available from Hennepin County Attorney's Office, Sexual Assault Services, C-2100 Government Center, Minneapolis, MN 55487.

Take Care with Yourself: A Young Person's Guide to Understanding, Preventing and Healing from the Hurts of Child Abuse (1983) Intermediate & Up
Laurie White and Steven Spencer
Designed to underscore the importance of self-worth, this book talks about people's motivations in situations of abuse and tells where to go to seek help. Available from Take Care With Yourself, 915 Maxine Ave, Flint, MI 48503.

Top Secret: Sexual Assault Information for Teenagers Only (1982)
Jennifer Fay and Billie Jo Flerchinger
Provides sexual assault information with an emphasis on self-protection. Available from King County Rape Relief, 305 S 43rd St, Renton, WA 98055.

A Very Touching Book (1983) Intermediate
Jan Hindman
Colorful illustrations are used to demonstrate good and bad touching. Proper names for genitalia are taught. Available from McClure-Hindman Books, PO Box 208, Durkee, OR 97905.

FOR ADULTS

The Best Kept Secret: Sexual Abuse of Children (1980)
Florence Rush
McGraw-Hill, NY
Gives an historical overview of the problem of child sexual abuse.

Come Tell Me Right Away: A Positive Approach to Warning Children about Sexual Abuse (No Date)
Linda Sanford
The Silent Children, also by Sanford, is summarized in booklet form. Available from Linda Sanford, 123 Sutherland Rd, Brookline, MA 02146.

The Common Secret: Sexual Abuse of Children and Adolescents (1984)
Ruth S. and C. Henry Kempe
W.H. Freeman and Co., NY
Provides both facts and insights for professionals who become involved in helping sexually abused children.

The Educator's Guide to Preventing Child Sexual Abuse (1986)
Mary Nelson and Kay Clark, Eds.
Network Publications, Santa Cruz, CA
Written to offer professionals an overview of current issues in the area of child sexual abuse. Well-known experts in the field are contributing authors. Available from Network Publications, ETR Associates, 1700 Mission St, Suite 203, PO Box 1830, Santa Cruz, CA 95061-1830.

HE TOLD ME Not to Tell! (1979)
The important points of Adams's *No More Secrets* are presented here in summary form. Available from King County Rape Relief, 305 S 43rd St, Renton, WA 98055.

I Never Told Anyone: Writings by Women Survivors of Child Sexual Abuse (1983)
Ellen Bass and Louise Thornton, Eds.
Harper Colophon Books
Personal testimonies of adult survivors of child sexual abuse offer comfort to others who have lived through the trauma.

Incest Annotated Bibliography (1984)
Meloyde L.F. Dabney, Ed.
University Press, University of Oregon, Eugene, OR
Annotated bibliography of 300 sources current through 1982. Available from Meloyde L.F. Dabney, 2000 Hawkins Ln, Eugene, OR 97405.

No More Secrets: Protecting Your Child from Sexual Assault (1981)
Caren Adams and Jennifer Fay
Impact Publishers, San Luis Obispo, CA
Suggestions for games to prevent sexual abuse, symptoms to look for if abuse is suspected, and steps to take if it has occurred are all contained in this book.

Questions Teachers Ask about Legal Aspects of Reporting Child Abuse (1984)
Cynthia Crosson Tower, Ed.
National Education Association Publication
Written in a question and answer format, this book contains a compilation of the child abuse reporting requirements for teachers nationwide. Available from Network Publications, ETR Associates, 1700 Mission St, Suite 203, PO Box 1830, Santa Cruz, CA 95061-1830.

The Safe Child Book (1985)
Sherryll Kerns Kraizer
Dell
A guide for parents in developing their children's own natural defense system against being sexually abused.

Sexual Abuse Prevention Education: An Annotated Bibliography (1985)
Kay Clark, Compiler
An annotated listing of over 200 items on the subject of child sexual abuse, with most materials published since 1980. Available from Net-

work Publications, ETR Associates, 1700 Mission St, Suite 203, PO Box 1830, Santa Cruz, CA 95061-1830.

Sexual Exploitation of Children (1985)
Daniel S. Campagna and Donald Poffenberger
Privately Published
This comprehensive manual is designed to give practitioners a look at child sexual exploitation through a diverse variety of viewpoints. Available from Daniel S. Campagna, 25 Berkshire Ave, Southwick, MA 01077.

The Silent Children: A Book for Parents about Prevention of Child Sexual Abuse (1982)
Linda T. Sanford
McGraw-Hill, NY
Divided into two sections. The first provides information and activities designed to help parents teach prevention; the second contains essays on the topic.

Strategies for Free Children: A Guide to Child Assault Prevention (1983)
Sally Cooper
For use in starting a child abuse prevention program. Designed for anyone who works with children to use when teaching them simple techniques to minimize their vulnerability. Available from Child Abuse Prevention Project, PO Box 02084, Columbus, OH 43202.

Talking about Sexual Abuse (1985)
Cornelia Spelman
Pamphlet which gives advice to parents on discussing sexual abuse with their children and also includes advice to adults who were molested as children. Available from National Committee for Prevention of Child Abuse and Neglect, 332 S Michigan Ave, Suite 1250, Chicago, IL 60604.

Three in Every Classroom: The Child Victim of Incest What You as a Teacher Can Do (1984)
Soukup, Wickner, Corbett
Richards Publishing Co., Gonvick, MN
Especially written to attune the educator to his/her role in helping the abused child. Available from Network Publications, ETR Associates, 1700 Mission St, Suite 203, PO Box 1830, Santa Cruz, CA 95061-1830.

Touch and Sexual Abuse (1984)
Illusion Theater
Minneapolis, MN
Designed as a guide for adults who need to talk to children about sexual abuse. Contains tips on what to say and what to look for if abuse is suspected. Available from Network Publications, ETR Associates, 1700 Mission St, Suite 203, PO Box 1830, Santa Cruz, CA 95061-1830.

Understanding Sexual Abuse (1982)
Gary May
Defines the different types of sexual abuse and sketches a profile of offenders. Available from National Committee for the Prevention of Child Abuse and Neglect, 332 S Michigan Ave, Suite 1250, Chicago, IL 60604.

Why Me? Help for Victims of Child Sexual Abuse (Even If They Are Adults Now) (1984)
Lynn B. Daugherty
Mother Courage Press, Racine, WI
An attempt to help adult victims of child sexual abuse come to terms with their feelings.

Your Children Should Know (1983)
Flora Colao and Tamar Hosansky
Bobbs-Merrill, NY
A good source book for both building children's defenses through practical exercises and offering advice to children and adults in surviving the trauma of child sexual abuse.

Appendix B:
Audiovisual Materials

The following is a list of recent audiovisual materials compiled from catalogs and reviews of the materials. They are for use by both adults and children.

Better Safe than Sorry (1978) Intermediate/Middle. FilmFair Communications, 10900 Ventura Blvd, Studio City, CA 91604 (213) 985-0244.
Sexual abuse by strangers and ways to prevent it are discussed in frank terms. All formats, 14½ min.

Better Safe than Sorry II (1982) Primary. FilmFair Communications, 10900 Ventura Blvd, Studio City, CA 91604 (213) 985-0244.
Teaches a 1, 2, 3 strategy in avoiding or dealing with sexual abuse. All formats, 14½ min.

Breaking the Silence (1986) Adults. Walt Disney Educational Media Co., 500 S Buena Vista St, Burbank, CA 91521 (800) 423-2555.
Identifies symptoms of child sexual abuse and offers guidelines for appropriate response. Stresses the importance of reporting the situation. All formats, 20 min.

Bubbylonian Encounter: A Film for Children about the Sense of Touch (1983) Primary/Intermediate. Kansas Committee for Prevention of Child Abuse, 435 S Kansas, 2nd Floor, Topeka, KS 66603 (913) 354-7738.
Adapted from the play by the same name, this film teaches the joys and perils of touch in an educational, entertaining context. 16mm, video, 27 min.

Child Molestation: A Crime Against Children (1982) Primary/Intermediate. AIMS Media, 6901 Woodley Ave, Van Nuys, CA 91406 (800) 367-2467.
Victims of child sexual abuse provide straight answers to questions posed about sexual molestation. 16mm, 11 min.

Child Sexual Abuse: What Your Children Should Know (1983) Indiana University Audio-Visual Center, Bloomington, IN 47405 (812) 335-8087.
Consists of 5 programs geared to meet the needs of each age group it addresses by arming adults and children with information and techniques to identify and to avoid sexual abuse. "A Program for Parents," 60 min.; K–3, 30 min.; Grades 4–7, 30 min.; Grades 7–12, 60 min.; and senior high, 60 min. Video.

Double Jeopardy (1978) Adults. MTI Teleprograms Inc., 108 Wilmot Rd, Deerfield, IL 60015 (800) 621-7870.
Emphasizes the callousness with which many sexual abuse victims are handled by community agencies and the legal system. Contrasts caring attitude of some professionals with belittling techniques of others. 16mm, 40 min.

If It Happens to You...Coping Strategies for Sexual Assault (1986) Intermediate/Middle. Sunburst Communications, 39 Washington Ave, Pleasantville, NY 10570–9971 (800) 431-1934.
A set of 2 "Trust Your Feelings," vignettes dramatize situations where sexual abuse can occur and "Be Assertive," which models specific suggestions and strategies to stop sexual advances. Urges victims to tell and offers guidelines on whom to tell. Video, 2 strips with cassettes, guide.

Never Say Yes to a Stranger (1985) Intermediate/Middle. MTI Teleprograms Inc., 108 Wilmot Rd, Deerfield, IL 60015 (800) 621-7870.
Vignettes, each followed by discussion, focus on safety tips and tactics to help children escape from strangers who might cause them harm. 16mm, video, 20 min.

No More Secrets (1982) Intermediate. O.D.N. Productions, 74 Varick St, Suite 304, New York, NY 10013 (212) 431-8923.
Dialog among 4 children educates viewers about abuse. 16mm, video, 13 min.

Now I Can Tell You My Secret (1985) Intermediate. Walt Disney Educational Media Co., 500 S Buena Vista St, Burbank, CA 91521 (800) 423-2555.
Uses the story of a young boy who has been molested and is keeping a secret to urge children to say no and to report any attempts at abuse. All formats, 15 min.

Some Secrets Should Be Told (1982) Primary/Intermediate. MTI Teleprograms Inc., 108 Wilmot Rd, Deerfield, IL 60015 (800) 621-7870.
Identifying sexual abuse and how to distinguish it from normal love and affection is demonstrated by Susan Linn and her puppets. 16mm, guide, 12 min.

Strong Kids, Safe Kids: A Family Guide (1984) Parents and children. Available at most home video stores.
Hosted by Henry Winkler, this video teaches children the basics in rebuffing sexual advances. Video, 43 min.

Touch (1984) Primary/Intermediate. MTI Teleprograms Inc., 108 Wilmot Rd, Deerfield, IL 60015 (800) 621-7870.
Film version of a theatrical presentation, this explores the different kinds of touch and what to do if touching turns abusive. 16mm, video, 32 min.

What Tadoo (1985) Preschool/Primary. MTI Teleprograms Inc., 108 Wilmot Rd, Deerfield, IL 60015 (800) 621-7870.
Young children are taught 4 basic rules to protect themselves from strangers when a young boy travels to the fantasy world of "Land of Lessons." 16mm, video, 18 min.

Who Do You Tell? (1980) Primary/Intermediate. MTI Teleprograms Inc., 108 Wilmot Rd, Deerfield, IL 60015 (800) 621-7870.
Offers advice on who to tell in case of abuse or other threatening situations. 16mm, 11 min.

Yes You Can Say No (1985) Upper Primary/Intermediate. The Committee for
Children, 172 20th Ave, Seattle, WA 98122 (206) 322-5050.
Development of assertive skills are modeled by David, a 10-year-old,
who learns to successfully handle a situation of exploitive touching.
Video, 19 min.

Appendix C:
Organizations and Agencies

Immediate referral to an agency in a specific geographic location is best accessed by dialing the *National Child Abuse Hotline* toll-free number: *(800) 4 A CHILD = (800) 442-4453*. The voluminous number of these governmental agencies makes their listing here impractical.

The following is a list of the major organizations and agencies in the nation that offer assistance and support in the prevention and treatment of child sexual abuse.

American Humane Association (AHA), American Association for Protecting Children, 9725 E Hampden Ave, Denver, CO 80231 (303) 695-0811.
 • Aids in the creation and promotion of child protective services through program planning, education, training, and consultation.

C. Henry Kempe National Center for the Prevention and Treatment of Child Abuse and Neglect, 1205 Oneida St, Denver, CO 80220 (303) 321-3963.
 • Focuses on the development of treatment programs for abused children.
 • Catalog of materials and services available upon request.

Committee for Children, 172 20th Ave, Seattle, WA 98122 (206) 322-5050.
 • Nonprofit organization dedicated to the prevention of child abuse.
 • Special focus on the prevention of the sexual exploitation of children.
 • Sponsors school-based curriculum development, professional training, community education, and original research.
 • Publishes *Prevention Notebook*, a monthly newsletter, and *Connections in the Prevention of Child Sexual Abuse*, a quarterly publication.

ETR Associates, 1700 Mission St, Suite 203, PO Box 1830, Santa Cruz, CA 95061–1830 (408) 429-9822.
 • Private, nonprofit organization responsible for the coordination of programs involving family life, sexual abuse prevention, and family health.
 • Publishes *Preventing Sexual Abuse*, a quarterly newsletter compiling the latest in research and resources.
 • Catalog of publications available upon request from Publishing Cooperative, a branch of this agency that distributes materials produced by nonprofit private and public agencies.
 • Sponsors nationwide prevention education seminars.

Incest Survivors Resource Network, International (ISRNI), Friends Meeting House, 15 Rutherford Pl, New York, NY 10003 (516) 935-3031.

- Aids in helping incest survivors to form neighborhood support groups, refers survivors to groups in their area.
- Emphasizes public education through sponsoring workshops and promoting media activities.

International Society for the Prevention of Child Abuse and Neglect (ISPCAN), 1205 Oneida St, Denver, CO 80220 (303) 321-3963.
- Publishes *Child Abuse and Neglect: The International Journal.*
- Sponsors an international congress on child abuse and neglect every 2 years.

National Center on Child Abuse and Neglect (NCCAN), Children's Bureau, Administration for Children, Youth and Families, US Department of Health and Human Services (HHS), PO Box 1182, Washington, DC 20013 (301) 251-5157.
- Federal agency in the Department of Health and Human Services responsible for administering funds for child abuse prevention and treatment, research, and model projects.
- Operates NCCAN Child Abuse Clearinghouse that offers annotated computer printouts of documents on specific aspects of child abuse or neglect.

National Child Abuse Coalition (NCAC), 1125 15th St NW, Suite 300, Washington, DC 20005 (202) 293-7550.
- Composed of national organizations with major interests in the area of child abuse and prevention.
- Goals are to sustain national attention on the child abuse problem and coordinate activities among the agencies on a national basis.
- Informs member organizations of federal legislation relating to child abuse.
- Information concerning federal legislation is available upon request from the coordinator.

National Committee for the Prevention of Child Abuse (NCPCA) 332 S. Michigan Ave, Suite 950, Chicago, IL 60604–4357 (312) 663-3520.
- Volunteer-based organization of private citizens working with community, state, and national groups to educate and inform the public about child abuse prevention.
- Chapters located throughout the United States.
- Catalog of publications available upon request.
- Publications that can be ordered from this catalog include an information and resources directory on child abuse, an annotated list of materials on child sexual abuse prevention resources, and a sex abuse prevention comic book for use with children, "Spider-Man & Power Pack."

Parents United/Daughters and Sons United/Adults Molested as Children United (AMACU), PO Box 952, San Jose, CA 95108 (408) 280-5055.
- National self-help organization with chapters located throughout the United States.
- Parents United offers assistance to families involved in child sexual abuse and sponsors support groups for child victims (Daughters and Sons United) and for adults who were child victims (Adults Molested as Children).
- Sponsors the Institute for the Community as Extended Family, which trains professionals in establishing child abuse treatment programs.

Subject Index

Compiled by Linda Webster

denial, 56
ethical considerations in
treatment, 168–69
etiology of sexual desires, 158–59
exploitation of child's need for
physical contact, 23
feelings about attraction to
children, 157
feelings of, 55–56
fixated offenders, 143–47
former victims, 148–49, 159–60
imprisonment, 142, 152–53, 164
incriminating statements used in
court cases, 124
known to child victim, 32, 38–39
legal system, 55–56, 130–31
likelihood of pleading guilty, 120
looking for children who will
cooperate, 32–33
motivations, 147–48
myths, 141–42
prosecution versus rehabilitation,
117
regressed offenders, 143–47, 157
sex drive reduction, 165–68
sexual sadism, 157
strangers as offenders, 22–23,
37–38
surgery, 164–65
treatment, 149–53, 163–69
Child protective services, 91, 98,
104, 105, 129, 134–35
Child rapists, 142–43. *See also*
Rapists
Child sexual abuse. *See also* Incest;
Prevention
audiovisual materials, 182–84
barriers to prosecution, 115–18
behavioral indicators, 24, 28, 47,
62–63, 96–97, 103, 109–10,
132
books about, 41–45, 175–81
defense mechanisms of victims,
72–80
definition, 54–55, 101–02, 115,
130
diagnosis of through play
technique, 108–13
failures in child protective
system, 129–36
media coverage, 10–11, 13

myths, 38
organizations and agencies,
185–86
parental role when child reports,
28–29
physical and behavioral signs, 47
physical indicators, 103
problems with statistics, 4
reporting requirements, 11, 29,
86–87, 91–92, 105–06, 132
self-defense techniques, 36–40
statistics, 5–7, 9–10, 23, 30, 38,
102, 112, 115
substantiation of child's story,
54–65
surveys, 5–7
underreporting of, 9
versus fantasies, 57–59, 116–17
victimization by peers, 74, 79
Child Sexual Abuse Treatment
Program, 13–14
Child victims. *See also* Incest
victims
alternatives to court appearance,
119–20
behavioral indicators, 24, 28, 47,
62–63, 96–97, 103, 109–10,
132
believability, 28, 57, 97, 116–18,
131–32
coercion used by offenders,
38–39, 55
court appearance, 114–28
court testimony not advisable,
124–25
defense mechanisms, 72–80
fears, 34, 63
guidelines for support of, 77,
78–79, 97–99
imposition of sex play on other
children, 97, 102
interviewing guidelines, 57–59,
104–05
parental reactions to abuse,
28–29, 102
physical indicators, 47, 103
psychological problems, 102
reactions when abuse is
discovered, 28, 102
removal from home, 133
revealing abuse, 28–29, 59, 61